W9-BWA-548

TRANSFORMATIONAL LEADERSHIP

TRANSFORMATIONAL LEADERSHIP

Conversations with the
Leadership Conference of Women Religious

Edited by Annmarie Sanders, IHM

ORBIS BOOKS
Maryknoll, New York 10545

ORBIS BOOKS
Maryknoll, New York 10545

Fathers and Brothers
MARYKNOLL™

Founded in 1970, Orbis Books endeavors to publish works that enlighten the mind, nourish the spirit, and challenge the conscience. The publishing arm of the Maryknoll Fathers and Brothers, Orbis seeks to explore the global dimensions of the Christian faith and mission, to invite dialogue with diverse cultures and religious traditions, and to serve the cause of reconciliation and peace. The books published reflect the views of their authors and do not represent the official position of the Maryknoll Society. To learn more about Maryknoll and Orbis Books, please visit our website at www.maryknollsociety.org.

Copyright © 2015 by the Leadership Conference of Women Religious

Published by Orbis Books, Box 302, Maryknoll, NY 10545-0302.

Manufactured in the United States of America

Library of Congress Cataloging-in-Publication Data

Transformational leadership : conversations with the Leadership Conference of Women Religious / edited by Annmarie Sanders, IHM.
    pages cm
  ISBN 978-1-62698-138-6 (pbk.)
  1. Christian leadership. 2. Contemlation. 3. Women clergy. 4. Leadership Conference of Women Religious of the United States. I. Sanders, Annemarie, editor. II. Leadership Conference of Women Religious of the United States.
BV625.1.T735 2015
255'.9—dc23

2015004811

CONTENTS

PREFACE

In 2009, the Leadership Conference of Women Religious (LCWR) suddenly gained the attention of the world when the Vatican announced two investigations of U.S. Catholic sisters. The first was an apostolic visitation through which the Vatican would seek information about the "quality of life" within all apostolic orders of U.S. sisters. Following on the heels of that news was the announcement of a second investigation. This one was a doctrinal assessment of LCWR, an organization of more than fourteen hundred Catholic sisters who head more than three hundred orders of sisters in the United States.

News of the doctrinal assessment by the Vatican's Congregation for the Doctrine of the Faith (CDF) piqued the curiosity of the media and society at large. What was LCWR and what had it done to warrant such a serious investigation? As reporters, researchers, scholars, and others probed LCWR's history and current work for signs of dissent and/or scandal, the initial interest in controversy turned more into an inquisitiveness about LCWR's mission, philosophy, and practices. Of particular interest to many was the way LCWR as an organization, as well as its members, exercised leadership. People noted marked differences between the way women religious practice leadership and the way it is often practiced by leaders in government, civic organizations, and churches, as well as in workplaces and professional organizations. Attention again turned to this way of leadership when the Vatican made a surprising announcement on April 16,

2015, that it had brought its assessment of LWCR to comple-
tion and released a concluding report jointly prepared by CDF
and LCWR. The report noted, "From the beginning, our extensive conversations were marked by a spirit of prayer, love
for the Church, mutual respect, and cooperation. We found
our conversations to be mutually beneficial." Such a positive
conclusion to what seemed to be an almost impossible stand-
off again drew the interest of the public. How did the resolution come about? What could be learned from this situation
about working through polarization? Repeatedly people expressed a hunger to learn more about the way of leading and
being in the world practiced by women religious and LCWR
that seemed effective and attractive.

So intense was the interest among a group of women and
men in the Washington, DC, area that they organized a conference to explore the type of leadership they were witness-
ing in LCWR and among its members. Held under the
auspices of the Institute for Policy Research and Catholic
Studies at The Catholic University of America, and entitled
"Spiritual Leadership for Challenging Times," the conference
sought to help lay women and men explore for themselves the
qualities or elements of the way of leadership unfolding
among women religious.

Conference keynoter Marie McCarthy, SP, associate director of programs for LCWR, authored an article based on
key concepts in her conference address.* Attempting to define
the kind of leadership being practiced by LCWR and its members, she described it as "more than a style, not nearly as pre-
cise, orderly, and straightforward as a model, [something that]
might best be spoken of as a way of being in the world." She
went on to say, "The best language I can find to name this
kind of leadership is 'transformational leadership,' that is, a set
of dispositions, a way of being in the world that, when fostered

---

*Marie McCarthy, SP, "Tending the Gifts in the Dark Places." *The Occa-
sional Papers*, Winter 2015, pp. 3–6.

in the leader, contributes to creating an environment in which deep, authentic transformation of the individual and of the whole is possible. It is a way of leadership that knows how to wait, how to endure, how to stay in the dark middle space tending to what can only mature in the darkness."

Marie continued, "It seems important to notice that women religious did not set out to develop a way of doing spiritual, transformational leadership. We set out to live our lives with authenticity, faithful to our call, rooted in prayer, and deeply grounded in gospel values. The particular way of leadership that has emerged among women religious is a direct result of that commitment. It is something we have grown into over time. It has unfolded among us step by step, in the concrete daily-ness of living. We didn't set out to go here but we can look back and see what has been taking shape."

In an effort to better understand this unfolding way of spiritual, transformational leadership, LCWR regularly conducts interviews on this topic with some of the most engaging and passionate contemporary thinkers. The interviews, which are published in LCWR's journal, *The Occasional Papers*, are part of LCWR's effort to explore the challenges of leadership from a faith perspective and assist its own members in navigating the tumultuous waters that so engulf leaders in these complex and ever-shifting times.

Transformational Leadership: Conversations with the Leadership Conference of Women Religious is a collection of eighteen of these interviews conducted over the course of several years by LCWR director of communications Annmarie Sanders, IHM. The interviewees—theologians, psychologists, educators, academics, authors, and leaders from various fields and disciplines—speak from their scholarship, professional knowledge, and, most important, their lived experience as seekers and searchers for a way of leadership able to meet the deep challenges of today's world.

The interviews selected for this collection explore topics critical to the practice of leadership for these times: how to refashion leadership in light of new realities; how to empower others to envision, adapt, and embrace change; how to lead an organization so that it can be an agent of transformation for the world; and how to encourage an organization to dream for its future and then adapt according to its dreams. These leaders share from their own experiences about leading through incidences of public trial and humiliation, managing situations of conflict and polarization, engaging their own inner resources when faced with tribulations, and living from a stance of deep contemplation.

Transformational Leadership: Conversations with the Leadership Conference of Women Religious offers the reader the opportunity to learn from such notables as Walter Brueggemann; Judy Cannato; Joan Chittister, OSB; Constance FitzGerald, OCD; Donald Goergen, OP; Marty Linsky; and Margaret Wheatley, as well as meet perhaps for the first time other leaders and thinkers filled with wisdom born of the experience of leading through challenging times.

Although addressed to Catholic sisters, the insights and wisdom shared in these interviews go far beyond this audience and have relevance for anyone exercising leadership. In addition, the reflective material and practical suggestions for living a Gospel-centered life make this collection of interest to all people seeking to live with purpose and depth, whether or not they are serving in a formal leadership role.

INTRODUCTION

By Pat Farrell, OSF

In my interactions with other members of the Leadership Conference of Women Religious (LCWR) I have often heard the comment that we are not living in a moment of "business as usual." Our time is one of enormous paradigm shift and increasing complexity. Some people have eyes to see it. Others seem more oblivious to the massive upheaval taking place on multiple levels. There are those who still deny global warming; who think that more frequent and serious world financial crises are simply a blip on the screen of normalcy; who hardly notice the increasing consumerism, greed, and fundamentalism, or see them as harmless exceptions to a more stable norm. When ways tried and true no longer seem to work, their tendency is to try harder to do more of the same, largely unaware of the futility of such striving.

I believe such persons to be a rapidly dwindling minority. There is increasing recognition that even the sources to which we typically turn for meaning—religious institutions, family constellations, educational establishments—are in crisis. Humanity is bumping up against the inadequacy of trusted institutions, cherished beliefs, worldviews, and philosophical constructs that are profoundly in jeopardy. Ours is a time of paradigm stress.

It is no coincidence that this moment in history has also engendered an unprecedented interest in mysticism and spirituality, suggesting both crisis and corresponding breakthrough that are transcendent in nature. There is talk of an evolution of consciousness, the birth of something new as the familiar fades. We catch glimpses of what is emerging, but a fresh future remains mostly hidden and poses numerous questions. Will the needed newness come as a painful emergence from darkness and ambiguity, a gradual dawning? Will it be costly grace, requiring intellectual rigor and spiritual asceticism in order for seekers to notice what lies beyond conventional, easily recognizable categories? Will it reveal itself as gratuitous gift, becoming visible perhaps when least expected? Will things get worse before they get better? How much human suffering will the process entail?

It is challenging to live with such uncertainty without the ennui that usually accompanies the absence of a compelling vision. The world is greatly in need of leaders who can give hope, inspire courage, and teach us to survive creatively an in-between moment. Leaders for such times are trapeze artists needing to let go, to be suspended in mid-air, and to trust that something to grasp will appear, carrying them toward a future not yet visible. Who can model such daring, such enlightened insecurity? Where are we to find leaders willing to risk, to release stale certitudes the human family has outgrown, to be suspended between what has been and what is not yet?

Catholic sisters who are elected leaders of their religious congregations have been asking similar questions as they face the challenges of guiding others in these transitional times. They were the primary audience for the interviews reprinted in this book. However, the perceptions and insights articulated here by a variety of contemporary wisdom figures speak to a much broader public. Transformational leadership is needed in all disciplines, all venues, all cultures and contexts. In this collection, wisdom articulated with a faith perspective is made accessible to readers in search of a fresh way forward. The authors name some of the essential tasks of effective leadership for uncertain times.

LCWR brings significant current experience into dialogue with the questions addressed in this book. Two areas in particular come to mind from the conference's recent history.

The first is the challenge of leadership in situations of polarization. The public questioning of women religious by Vatican officials in the form of the apostolic visitation of all U.S. women religious and the doctrinal assessment of LCWR reflected a breakdown in fruitful relationships and communication. It challenged LCWR members to particular care, discernment, and depth in determining how to respond to these investigations with integrity in a way that would not deepen the divide. With hindsight I am aware of important leadership learnings.

One discovery is that in moments of controversy, intense collective emotion clouds the view of effective solutions. Conflict needs the response of non-anxious leaders capable of calm, steady, quiet courage. It requires the skill of listening without judgment, naming without denial, exploring issues without predetermined solutions in mind. It needs an ever-growing capacity for relationship-building across the chasm of ego and fixed positions. The more intractable the differences appear to be, the greater the need to create space around them for something unexpected to emerge. Swiss Jungian psychologist Maria Louise von Franz states: "If we can stay with the tension of opposites long enough, sustain it, be true to it, we can sometimes become the vessels within which the divine opposites come together and give birth to a new reality."

A second relevant area of LCWR experience is the conference's ongoing promotion of contemplative practices and processes. It has occasioned a shift, a deepening in the dynamic of LCWR gatherings. The silence and emptiness of contemplative stillness spring from an intentional opening to Holy Mystery, an active attentiveness to deeper inner movements and other levels of perception. Darkness is then experienced as transformative. Personal and communal transformation is recognized as beyond effort, gratuitously given from the divine presence to which we can only make ourselves available.

Call it grace, conversion, ripening, healing, emergence: the world is in need of such unfolding from within. New visions for the future will come from a growing capacity to perceive what is in harmony with all that is, with the divine core in everything and everyone. As it is, the human tendency is to see reality not as it is, but as we are. Truly, the world around us gets better as we get better. Leaders who themselves have undergone a process of transformation are more able to provide leadership that is transformational. If you have this text in hand, you are likely a seeker of such transformation. May these interviews provide inspiration for living and leading with intentionality and depth, with authenticity, creativity, and faithfulness.

LEADERSHIP
AND CONTEMPLATION

1

The Role of Contemplation in Leadership

Marcia Allen, CSJ

Many people today acknowledge the need for leadership that is grounded deeply in the divine. But how might leaders make a serious commitment to a life of profound contemplation and lead from this space? How might that commitment be lived out in the everyday, practical duties of a leader? And why is it imperative to do so?

For greater insight into these questions, LCWR turned to **Marcia Allen, CSJ**, who has worked with women religious throughout the country, giving retreats and workshops and assisting in planning and facilitating meetings for religious communities. At the time of this interview she had just been elected president of her community. She later was elected LCWR president.

You have encouraged leaders to take a long, loving look at their own community, to gaze at it and linger with it until it allures them into it and they can see within it places of mysticism. You encourage them to hold their community contemplatively until they can see its vulnerability as well as their own vulnerability, until they can be at one with their community. Could you say more about what this practice might mean for a leader and for a community?

What I would say to leaders is the same thing I would say to anyone else, and that is what Karl Rahner said in the last century.

He said that the Christian of the future would either be a mystic or nothing at all. His definition of a mystic is one who can "see the mystery in anything and everything—in the everyday and the banal, as well as in the very extraordinary." So I think we must cultivate the ability to see the mystery in the open door, the doorknob, the empty shoe at the side of the bed, the face in the window, the ring of the phone. What is the mystery, and what keeps us from seeing it?

I think what the mystic has come to understand is that God and God's dynamic energy are present in all, around all, and through all. As theologian Anne Hunt says in her work, *What Are They Saying about the Trinity?* God is a personal dynamic that manifests itself in mutuality, reciprocity, creativity, and inclusion. As we make our way through our day and through our world, we learn to comprehend how this dynamic energy is at work in every moment and every day and every place, and how it is at work in us. It seems to me that we incarnate this energy. Where we are, this energy is at work. It is inhibited by our own blindness, our stubbornness, our own ignorance, but is also free to do its thing by our openness, our willingness, our competence, and our freedom to be at its disposal.

You also speak of taking the experiences that could make a leader mute—the very difficult as well as the exceedingly beautiful experiences—and becoming vulnerable before them so that the experiences might be agents of transformation. Could you speak more about how this kind of contemplation of life experiences can be transformative?

A mystic is available to and for the moment. So I believe that we are called to this kind of everyday awareness. We're called to an alertness that moves beyond the "stuckness" we feel in the overwhelming plethora of the trivia, the endless minor tasks that pile up on us day after day. We're called to see them as not something to get past, but as the mystery that life gifts us with at any particular day or hour. Each thing is a piece of the mystery of how God is acting in the world, and God, as Eckhart says, is from all eternity lying in labor giving birth. In every moment God's energy is acting or longing to act in favor of creation. The question for us is, "How will we cooperate with this gift?"

When we listen to what it is that God desires for the world and when we look upon the world in a spirit of complete openness, it can be risky. A contemplative stance can challenge us to move forward into the realm of possibilities without being all too sure of where we are going. What do you recommend to those seeking to live in a more contemplative stance but who feel afraid or too uncertain?

The Jesuit author André Lefèvre made an enormous impression on me when he described the biblical servant as one whose glad and practical cooperation with God is the manner in which that person goes about daily life—glad and practical cooperation with God and with anyone and anything that comes into one's day-to-day activities. The phone rings, the appointment is made, the article or letter is read, the meeting is held. We work with attorneys, money managers, members who are discerning a new ministry, who are distressed, or engaged in trying ministries, or who are dying. In every moment we enter into glad and practical cooperation with the energy with which God is bursting at the moment.

This I believe is the simple mysticism that Rahner called ordinary. It doesn't take long hours of contemplation, although I am certainly not discounting steady and regular prayer. It does take an attention to the moment and a resolution to remember the presence of God. This can become a habit of mind, a habit of soul; it becomes what Simone Weil calls "love." Love, she said, is not a state of the soul, love is a direction. This is, after all, what we signed up for when we made our commitment in religious life. Love, we acknowledged, was at the root of our longing, the direction in which we hoped to live out the rest of our life. It was the one thing necessary, and we recognize that God was at the bottom of it all. God was our one motivation. Hopefully, this motive has endured and borne fruit. Hopefully, by the time we are in elected leadership, we have committed ourselves over and over to this one source of our motivation. Hopefully, we understand our commitment as one of glad and practical participation in the project that is God. That is the desire that God has for creation—a fulfillment as it emerges and unfolds in our day-to-day world.

As communities of women religious are increasingly engaging the whole in decision-making, what is the role of communal contemplation? How can communal contemplation help us to envision new ways and new solutions that might be greater than what any one person could conceive?

Communal contemplation is indeed challenging, and it is often difficult to judge that this has happened. It seems to me that a community gathered with the intent to contemplate together some resolution or decision is enabled to do that through various technologies that facilitate a rhythm of quieting, conversation, and personal contemplation. Someone, I think it was Walter Brueggemann, said that conversation is speech that converts. Real conversation is one during which a participant can offer an idea, an insight, or an opinion and then turn loose of it, allowing others to engage with it and change it as they wish. It is welcoming ideas and insights of others and allowing oneself to be influenced by them. It's the art of real encounter. All of this is hard to come by, and it takes real discipline. It also requires consistent engagement at the conversational and contemplative level. This type of consistent engagement   requires commitment. Most community meetings are held so far apart that the participants forget what happened in the meeting prior to the one they are attending. At the same time, the meetings are generally so packed with necessity that there is only time to make decisions rather than take the time necessary to actually contemplate and converse.

How can leaders foster greater corporate exploration in their communities of the presence of God and the workings of God?

I believe that a communal decision to spend the time necessary to actually have contemplative conversation is necessary. A commitment to cooperate with one another in this way is vital. Various experts have designed technologies to assist communities in this work. For example, Parker Palmer's book, *Inner Wholeness*, Carl Frankel's book, *Out of the Labyrinth*, and, of course, Peter Senge's book, *Presence*, are three of the chief resources a community can use. They all attempt to enable communities to work toward sustainable conversations.

Sustainability is, I believe, the value that roots a community in rewarding conversation. Sustainability requires commitment, patience, openness, and real devotion to the project of becoming community—viable community in our day and age. It seems to me that this is the work of any religious community in our time. Sustained and open conversation that is contemplative in nature will enable us as religious communities to come to our truest vocation. Our time calls for community, communion; not just individual commitment but communal commitment. If love is the direction of the soul, then it is the communal soul that must commit to this direction. Most of us have all done what we need to do individually. Now is the time for communal effort. We must engage in and with our world as community, a work in process together, which is the meaning of community as signified by its Latin root.

In speaking of some of the overwhelming situations of the world, Constance FitzGerald, OCD, has said, "We give in to a passive sense of inevitability and imagination dies. Everything seems too complex, too beyond reach." Do you see this happening in U.S. religious life—a giving in to a sense that we can do nothing as religious to change the state of religious life? And, if so, is this in-hibiting our capacity to imagine something different?

Laurie Brink, OP, in the winter 2007 issue of *Horizon*, said something that sticks in my mind in some unyielding way. She suggests that religious communities of women have come to that mid-to-late-life stage in which the person has seen it all and done most of it and is now ready to relinquish the struggle—to settle in and down and relax for the long haul of getting old. This trend is sparked by the long tussle with re-newal that has seen only diminishment in institutional spon-sorship, the rise of individualism, middle-class comfort, professionalism and its inherent perks, and consumerism that is the by-product of our middle-class lifestyle. Brink portrays a life that no longer beckons to those who might have a call to make God the center of one's life.

What she describes is what I believe is the challenge for leadership and for communities today. Simone Weil says, "The only way not to suffer is to lapse into unconsciousness, and there are many who yield in one way or another to this temp-tation. To retain the lucidity, self-responsibility, and dignity appropriate to a human being means condemning oneself to a renewed fight every day against despair."

William Johnston, SJ, says that the world needs people whose very being reflects the conflicts and sufferings of the world. He says, "That world vibrates within them, they breathe its air, they feel its frustrations, they carry its cross." What does Johnston's claim have to say to those in religious life today and to leaders today?

Our commitment—personal and communal—the very pur-pose for the existence of our religious community, is to be pas-sionate about God and the things of God in the world in which they exist. Our world today calls us to what the theolo-gian Beverly Lanzetta names "an unmediated incommensurate condition." We are called to be face-to-face with the enormous suffering and the needs of our present era. The human condition, the Earth's conditions—all unmediated—are in our face, moment by moment. We have not the time to settle in and down, to be complacent, to reap the benefits of our early labors. No, we are invited to be present, to be face-to-face with our world, our planet.

We are committed, as is God, to the project that has been begun by God, but that needs us for its continued unfolding. We understand ourselves as incommensurate, the world as incommensurate. No one of us can measure up to the work that needs doing. As community we can show up to do it while recognizing that even as community we are not up to the task. However, it is in the togetherness of the effort within and among the community members, and their communion with others around them that the common work for the Earth's community begins to make sense. Continuous conversation, reaching out to one another and others, reveals the connectedness of all things. It honors the implicate order of all creation. This is the vision that the leader holds, and that which she consistently holds up for the community.

Is there anything else that you would like to say to summarize your insights into contemplation?

All of this is about committing to the mystery of life, the mystery of creation, the mystery of God. It's about believing and acting as if this single life, this leader's moment in time, and this community's moment in time is imperative for the implicate order. This is the contemplative task, the mystical task. It doesn't take long hours of silence and solitude. I'm not negating the necessity of personal silence and solitude; I'm simply trying to say that what we need is that awareness and alacrity that the mystical heart implies.

We know that it was this kind of heart that inspired the inception of each of our communities. We cannot renege on it now just because we think we are living in more complex and trying times. Our response must be a gladsome YES—the YES of consecration that Rahner speaks of. It is the YES when all our moments, past and future, fuse in the now. This YES is our commitment to the inclusive, mutual, reciprocal, and creative dynamic that is constantly at birth within and around us. It is our abandonment to practical cooperation with God who is birthing moment to moment.

If this sounds too idealistic, if the day is too packed with activity to remember it, if we are too cynical to believe it, then we are challenged to ask ourselves: What is the real responsibility of leadership?

Every Passion Sunday we hear the reading from Isaiah, chapter 50, that goes something like this: I have given you a well-trained tongue that you might speak to the weary a word that will rouse them. This is the work of leadership. To articulate the insights, the ideals of community, the communal forum, the communal energy so that the community understands its guiding energy and its guiding work in and for creation. Yes, it takes a mystic's imagination and a mystic's vision to understand that mystery is everywhere and in everything, only waiting to be recognized and acknowledged. To be a mystic is to anticipate mystery, to recognize it, and to respond to it in the moment.

The work is simple, actually. We are the ones who complicate it with our need for space and time. All we really need is a passion for God. God will do the rest. This takes us back to contemplation. With open eyes we see our world. With an open heart we embrace our world. Through the day-to-day routine that surrounds us, we give ourselves with open ears and open arms to the guiding work of bringing to birth with glad and practical cooperation whatever it is that lies before us.

2

Pursuing Our Dreams in Times of Darkness

Constance FitzGerald, OCD

At the time of this 2006 interview, **Constance FitzGerald, OCD**, was prioress of the Carmelite Monastery in Baltimore, where she also has been director of formation, treasurer, and archivist. A contemplative theologian, she has lectured extensively throughout the world on her explication and interpretation of the great Carmelite mystics. She is well known for her work on John of the Cross and Teresa of Avila, and particularly for her interpretation of the dark night in relation to contemporary life and society.

The Carmelite Monastery in Baltimore had become known for how it squarely faced the reality of its decline, envisioned a different future, and took the steps to turn the members' dreams into reality. LCWR wished to learn how a leader can effectively engage members in a process of collective dreaming. How does a leader create a climate for dreaming? How does one continue to dream through darker and more difficult times?

Your Carmelite community has had a long history of dreaming for its future and adapting itself according to those dreams. Can you describe the place of dreaming in your community?

The foundation and the object of my community's dreaming is the life of prayer, the contemplative life. While our dreams have more concrete and practical objects, they are of a piece with the central goal of union with God, communion with God and all creation. More specifically, the heart of my dream and my community's dream has been the reinterpretation of the Carmelite tradition for the times in which we live. In other words, we want to offer a contemporary interpretation that is accessible, comprehensible, and relevant for people so that this ancient mystical tradition might serve as both guide and stimulus for a deeper spiritual life. This dream is the basis for everything that we have done, and it has guided all our practical decisions about our contemplative life.

Can you give an example of a successful process of dreaming in your recent history?

We had a dream as a community about eight years ago to have new members, and we made this dream our primary objective. We were a very strong contemplative community but we knew that we had five to ten years to attract new members or we would be finished—not right away, but during that time span we would grow too old to educate new members into the tradition.

So we began to imagine how to achieve this objective, and we engaged everyone in the community in the process. We divided the community into five age groups and asked them what they might be able to contribute to the life and formation of new members. Each age group came back with definite ideas of what they could offer to attract younger women to the community and to support them so they would persevere. And, more significantly, each group has been able to follow through with its specific contribution and commitments. As it worked out, this process affected a profound conversion in the sisters that transformed the whole community. Following Vatican II with its mandate for renewal and adaptation, we came into some good, legitimate freedoms and they are still valuable. However, it was necessary to make concrete sacrifices of some of these freedoms for the sake of our dream. A kind of self-transcendence had to take place in order to welcome the new people. For example, I have put aside much of my writing and lecturing, since I cannot give my attention to those demands and be fully present for the formation of our newer members. Also, each sister had to become more open to different perspectives, bear with the tensions of an ongoing re-forming of the community with each entrant, and consciously provide a place for new members, and this involved difficult forfeitures.

Some groups may decide that these costs are too high or impossible, but new members are not going to persevere if the community is not prepared to make significant personal sacrifices. This is all part of dreaming; there are consequences. In order to realize dreams, one must be ready to pay a price. We made these sacrifices for the sake of a passion and a cause that was greater than any one of us. Now with six new members (a third of our community), our older members are at their very best, determined to pass on our rich Carmelite tradition in a deeply bonded community that walks into the future with hope.

In the years of renewal, your community began to dream of something new and different. What were the inspirations and influences that helped you bring your dreams into reality?

Vatican II was certainly the critical moment that provided the climate for our new dream. The theology of the Council documents gave us an impetus to start moving forward in a new direction. We were prepared for this moment by a number of influences, significant among them the freedom and flexibility of heart that has characterized our community since its beginnings in 1790. This flexibility provided a seed bed for envisioning concrete changes. Also our rootedness in history and tradition gave us a strong identity and self-assurance so that we had the courage to try new things. We sensed that our roots were too deep to be pulled up by the process of experimentation. I think that the fear of loss of identity has short-circuited the re-visioning process in many communities, ironically leading to the very thing feared—deterioration in the sense of identity, purpose, and mission, and often even a lukewarmness that can discourage new members. But communities that are unafraid to reinterpret their charism will discover in their communal soul a new passion and enlivened sense of who they are, even while maintaining a continuity with the past. We, on our part, have derived a great strength and deepened experience of identity from the long years of growth and struggle, and for this reason we now have an even greater capacity to dream.

Education and study also played a role in our dreaming. I cannot overstate their importance in giving religious women the tools, the wisdom, the insight, and the courage necessary both to imagine new dreams and to bring those dreams into reality. One cannot dream or imagine out of a vacuum; the imagination has to be fed, the dreaming function must be nourished. For example, the biblical renewal in the 1950s and '60s was a vital influence on me, along with extensive reading of the existentialist philosophers and of the theologians who became dominant in the Council. After Vatican II our entire community studied the theology of the Council documents, through which we became ever more aware of what needed to change and why. We began to dream for ourselves. Education and study help a community to be ready when the moment for decisive action arrives. But the preparation time can be clouded in obscurity since, at the time, we do not always know the ultimate purpose that awaits us.

In addition to education and study, communities need to have at least a few individuals with exceptional imaginative capacity who can integrate all the input of a community and envision a changed future. Imagination is the integrating function that allows us to take the tradition and enliven it with new insight. It is critical to have people who can grab hold of this, who can bring together all the thinking, all the

work. This does not mean that they are the only ones visioning, but they are facilitating the emergence of a communal
dream.

Often a failure at dreaming and visioning reduces to a failure of imagination and a failure of knowledge, and conse-
quently, fear becomes operative. What has most helped my
community in this respect is that we have developed a communal habit of dreaming, very grounded in contemplative
prayer and in our identity.

*Could you talk more about the habit of dreaming and what that
looks like?*

As part of the renewal process we engaged in a leadership
training program in the early 1970s that included as a core element dreaming from the contemplative posture. In this program we learned to approach our decision-making and
questions by asking: "What would it be like if...?" This
process, now well established and deeply rooted, helps us give
voice to our most creative dreams, whether or not they are
achievable or initially practical. From these imaginative expressions, which always sort of knock down the borders, we are
able to identify our assumptions, as well as both the worst and
best possibilities, and then set concrete goals and objectives.
This process is now so incorporated into our community life
that it can truly be called a habit of dreaming. I think that the
community realizes it has never arrived and that we always
continue to look at new possibilities for ourselves.

*What has it been like to bring your community's dreams to
fruition?*

The process is something like being a patient gardener. We
have had to learn to plant the dream and then wait for the
seed to grow. This approach has generally led to planning that
is progressive, incremental, thoughtful, and unrushed.

Prophetic changes demand this patient waiting, since everybody cannot just latch onto a dream as soon as they hear about it. Moreover, each dream needs extended personal and communal reflection and discernment. The process of germination is incredibly important.

How do you continue dreaming during times when there seems to be little hope, during times of darkness?

Dreaming during times of darkness will demand much of us and on many different levels. We can get some guidance from the elements that brought our dreams to reality in the past, and we can draw from the heart of the contemplative tradition. A firm grounding in contemplative prayer is the only way to keep new visions from being just irresponsible dreaming into the future. Contemplative prayer is also the way through the intense darkness that we experience today, particularly with the institutional church. This darkness can be terribly destructive and can lead us to despair, but the contemplative mindset can see it also as an opportunity for transformation and the place where the deepest kind of hope can be born.

How can we distinguish between authentic hope and mere optimism?

Authentic theological hope is distinguished from mere optimism by the belief that without the surrounding darkness and seeming hopelessness, transformation really does not happen. We are talking about the kind of transformation that is largely hidden from our view. The vision that we continue to long for is actually dependent upon such times of darkness.

This insight from contemplative development can help to conceptualize the process of dreaming and visioning in darkness. In such times, it is critical that we learn to understand, dream, and vision by looking at and bearing with our unknowing, our blockages, and our blindness. We vision specifically by sustaining the darkness. This is contemplation in its deepest sense, where one's search for truth and vision is given over to mystery.

How can times of darkness help communities reimagine religious life and dream new dreams?

We need to be truly contemplative people who recognize that in darkness and obscurity God can put together all the material we have accumulated for new dreams and a new future, if we hold a receptive posture that will allow this integration to take place. John of the Cross speaks of the purification of memory that can and must happen in this profound darkness in order for a new vision to break through. We all project from our past into our future, and some of that is good. But some of it can hold us back. This is where theological hope comes into the picture. Theological hope is an openness in obscurity to the unimaginable possibilities of God, possibilities that are not restricted by a mere projection of our own past. Ironically, this openness comes only when we fear that we are at our end, with no human hope in sight, and we do not know what to do.

In reimagining religious life and dreaming new dreams from a place of darkness, we will have to be ready to let go of our preconceived notions. This might mean letting go of our ideas of the size of religious communities, external practices, or specific expressions of the life that have developed, in order to consider other alternatives that could emerge. The process is largely a passive one that we can cooperate with only by becoming ever more contemplative. This cooperation is a kind of self-transcendence, which is the key to transformation, and which leads ultimately to the release of the imagination's creative powers. It is a very difficult process to believe in, yet it is what has happened in the past and what is happening now in communities and with individuals. People are at all different stages of this contemplative process.

How can we discern between our own dreams and hopes and what might be God's dreams and hopes? In other words, how can we be utterly attentive to God's dream and not let our ego get in the way?

If we are living a deep life of prayer then we will be led slowly to move beyond our own projections, beyond our own memories of the past, and beyond thinking that the future has to be like the past. As I said earlier, John of the Cross calls this a purification of memory. This is how we become really free, meaning more and more unencumbered.

How do you think that individuals and congregations can best move forward through this process?

Ongoing education is key. Religious women need to continue to read, learn, and appropriate new materials. This is the food for new dreams and new visions. As I suggested earlier, creative and contemplative processes require intense periods of input, time for preparing the ground before we even know what will be sown there. While the philosophers and theologians of the 1940s, '50s, and '60s offered important influences for the last renewal, today we need to look to science and religion, quantum physics, evolution, ecology, and the implications of the new cosmology for theology and life. While we may not be able to become experts in all these fields, it is essential that we be familiar with the general concepts and vision of the universe that are at the core of these disciplines. We need to prepare ourselves now for a time when more specific action is needed, for the time when our dreams mature. So, on the one hand, there is the passive process of contemplative darkness, but, on the other, there is this very active part of education and preparation.

I also believe that we should not be too ready to die. While we need to accept the possibility of a future without us, it seems to me that many communities are too willing to accept their demise. As for my own community, I am simply determined that it will go on. I am not going to let this community that is 216 years old stop, and I am prepared to give everything for this one priority. Now, I do recognize that at a certain point it may be too late for some communities to recover. But I think that until that point there can be hope for something new to emerge, provided that we dedicate our full energies to the task—both actively and passively in prayer.

Furthermore, we need to be open to experimentation and avoid the fear of losing our identity. If we are to be capable of dreaming new dreams, we will need a continuing openness to new ways, without allowing fear to paralyze us. Religious identity will not be lost so long as those who dream and imagine have solid education, knowledge, and experience of the community's traditions and charism and are grounded in prayer.

Lastly, we have to be dedicated to transmitting the communal spirit. It will take tireless work to pass on the essence of our respective traditions to the next generation. I am convinced that religious life is now entering upon another stage of renewal; the one we have lived for the last forty years following Vatican II is over. But this new stage must hold a continuity with the past even while transcending it.

What can congregations who feel overwhelmed by this kind of visioning do?

Not every community will be able to take religious life forward into a new vision. But it may be that if even a few can make the leap, they will draw the others over the border or over the horizon with them. It may be that one community can fill an important dreaming function for the others. Even those communities that cannot possibly imagine taking forward a viable expression of their life may take hope in the possibility, however unimaginable right now, that they will be brought over the border by others if they remain contemplatively open to this movement. This means that collaboration among religious communities will continue to be essential.

I think that, finally, we have to wait patiently. The contemplative process of prayer tells us that when we surrender to darkness and come to a place of authentic theological hope we may have to wait still longer for knowledge, a new kind of knowledge that allows us to see in a radically transformed way. A vision of religious life fit for the time, a new perspective, may come later, possibly much later. We need to be prepared to bear with the obscurity and to live happily and healthily with hope until the vision emerges.

3

Integrating Contemplative Practices into Leadership

Nancy Sylvester, IHM

 *How might we understand contemplation as a way of being and how might leaders cultivate the dispositions and attitudes needed to be contemplative and lead contemplatively? What might it mean for an organization to become contemplative and why would organizations benefit from this approach?*

LCWR asked **Nancy Sylvester, IHM**, to address the need for and ways to integrate contemplative practices into leadership. The founder and president of the Institute for Communal Contemplation and Dialogue, as well as the sponsor of Engaging Impasse: Circles of Contemplation and Dialogue®, she is a past LCWR president and a former researcher, lobbyist, and national coordinator of NETWORK, a national Catholic social justice lobby.

Why do you believe that religious life leadership today needs to be approached from a contemplative perspective?

We are in such an incredible time in the evolution of the species. We are breaking into a new mode of consciousness. In the last fifty years we have experienced amazing breakthroughs in terms of civil rights, women's rights, psychology, quantum physics, and the new Universe Story to mention a few. Each has invited us to see ourselves differently as interdependent and part of the Earth community. We have moved into such new understandings that we find ourselves dealing with many significant issues of culture, meaning, and identity, and they cannot be addressed in the typical ways of discourse.

We are addressing issues that have to do with God, the Eucharist, theology, membership, and the future of religious life, and we need to do it in new ways. It is a reality that the religious life that we have known, loved, and cherished is coming to an end, so we have major issues of identity and meaning to face. Because there is no one answer we need a way to engage one another that comes out of the deep wellsprings of our own spirituality. For me that is a contemplative approach.

We don't know what the future is, and we can face that fact with an attitude of depression or excitement. We can feel excited because, in the last fifty years, women religious have been engaging with the breakthroughs in society from a rootedness in prayer and the Spirit. Even in the midst of all the changes, the one constant is that we are women of prayer. If we could harness that energy and be more intentional about opening ourselves up and being spacious, contemplative persons, and do that together, we could imagine new ways of responding to these difficult questions. We could contribute so much not only to the future of religious life but also to some of the critical issues of our planet.

How could engaging in leadership in a more contemplative way help congregations face these questions?

First I would say that we need to be careful in how we understand contemplation. I always cringe when people say something like, "Let's do contemplative leadership" as if it's the newest fad, or then, after they think they've experienced it, say, "We've tried that already," eager to move to something new. There is also a danger in trying to define how people should do contemplative leadership. Contemplation is a form of prayer, but it is also a way of being. Leaders can cultivate the dispositions and attitudes for a contemplative way of being and couple that with a variety of good processes and practical skills.

I'd prefer to advocate for the position that leaders need to look at the issues of grave consequence to us from a contemplative stance and integrate that practice into leadership.

How would you say this differs from the way we approached questions in the past?

Let's say that a person entered religious life in the 1950s. At that time, she could have taken the catechism of the church and said, "This is exactly what I believe." Today the members of most congregations would not have unanimity about those beliefs, or at least not without using quite a bit of extrapolation or refining of some of the language. Because of what we have experienced in terms of feminist understandings and what we have learned about the Universe Story, we are asking how the Christian story fits with all of this. Within most congregations there are women on the entire spectrum on these issues. How do we talk together? How do we begin to see one another's perspectives?

In the past we might have relied on outside authorities or intellectual debate to resolve these kinds of issues. Although there is still a place for that input, these issues touch our emotions and our psyche. They address our experience, and purely rational thinking cannot move us forward together.

The contemplative posture is one that opens us up to ambiguity, paradox, and the unknown because it releases for us a lot of our preconceived ways of being and thinking and it releases us of our ego. As we try to get in touch with the God within and become open to the Spirit, we are doing some of the very difficult inner work so essential if we are to respond in new ways.

What's the advantage for a leadership team to cultivate a contemplative approach intentionally?

When we engage in contemplation, we develop a welcoming heart and a way of listening to others that allows us to really hear and not just focus on what we think we should be hearing. When we engage in a contemplative stance we realize we are not in control and that we don't always have the best answer. That seems very simple, but it can be pretty hard when you are working with people, when you are hurried, or when you have to make decisions too quickly, as is often the case for leaders today. We don't always engage others' wisdom in such a way that something new might emerge. As we become more contemplative, we can hold the differences that we experience within our congregations, we can take people out of the boxes we have placed them in for years.

There is a lot that keeps us from uncorking or releasing our potential to think more creatively and differently. If we haven't been in touch with our own fears, compulsions, shadow, and ego we can keep the Spirit from generating through us new responses to some of our issues. I don't believe every issue that faces a leadership team has to be dealt with through an explicitly contemplative process, just as not everyone in an institute has to participate in every decision. We know after a while that this doesn't work. What is important is that each individual on a team needs to be cultivating a contemplative spirit so that as a team they can approach an issue in a contemplative way by taking a long, loving look at whatever question is at hand. Together a group can look upon the various facets of an issue and listen to all the voices speaking about that issue, even the ones saying exactly what we dislike. The key is how we listen to ourselves and listen to others.

You noted that we are approaching the end of religious life as we have known it. How does this impact the need to lead from a more contemplative approach?

I believe a contemplative approach will evoke new possibilities in us, especially if we start to do this together—as congregations or even as LCWR. Otherwise, we might just drift into a survival mode. If we are not aware of our own fears and can't release those fears in healthy ways, we are not going to have the energy to do something new, to move forward, to relinquish certain things so that the future can go on in new ways. Granted, facing our fears can be very uncomfortable. But, if we approach the future this way together, we hopefully will be strengthened.

What I have seen in my work with religious over these past years is that as we try to engage issues or situations of powerlessness in our lives together, we come to new understandings. Trust among us grows and we are awakened to some different ways of being that can change the situations we engage. Not that we necessarily go out and change the situation, but we change how we enter into it, how we respond to it, and how we are creating it. This new way of being makes a difference, and it invites a transformation of the individual, which can be a challenge.

I know that from my own life. I was someone who was very clear about positions and prone to take to the microphone and articulate my views. I would work hard to be sure things would go the way that I thought best. Now I find myself much more willing to hold more tentatively some of those opinions, to see from other perspectives. To allow this shift to occur, we have to be willing to change our behaviors a bit, as well as what people expect of us and what we expect of others. In religious life, we suffer from having put people in boxes for so long that we don't know how to experience one another in new ways.

What do you think holds people back from engaging in these more contemplative practices?

One thing is time. We don't give ourselves time for contemplation —either individually or collectively. It is probably the hardest thing to cultivate in leadership. It takes time to respond and not just to react to what is immediately before us. When we react, what often gets lost and goes unaddressed are the bigger questions such as: How are we dealing with grief in our congregations? How are our members dealing with insecurity? We, along with the whole country, are facing financial insecurity. How are we handling that? Are we reacting out of a stance of scarcity or responding from a stance of abundance?

Fear is another culprit, especially the fear that we are going to have to change. Some people simply choose not to change. Others, I think, have a misunderstanding of contemplation and fear that if they become too contemplative they will lose their passion for a work or for an issue. That is a legitimate concern, but I don't think it's valid. Mystics and contemplatives will say that true contemplation ends in action, and often the action is even more radical because it is being done with true freedom and comes with a purity of heart. In this sense, we act without any hidden agendas.

What are some examples of situations or questions that a congregation might want to explore collectively through a contemplative approach?

Our current culture keeps us separate and pits us against others, as we see in the political arena. Our call as religious is to show that there is another way to approach life. Given the complexity of these times, we need to look at an issue from its many sides. When discussions get coded in aggressive language and take place at a feverish pitch, it is very difficult to reflect and act from a stance of openness. This same dynamic can take place between congregation leaders and members. Our exchanges with one another can create tension levels that are so high that we need to step back and pause. That's when engaging in some contemplative sitting together can be very helpful. When we sit together in contemplation, we begin to soften. Our hearts soften as we welcome the other in. We become more spacious for the other person and for ourselves.

I think this is an approach we could take when we are looking at the areas in our lives where we feel powerless. For example, rather than just looking at the statistics on our congregation demographics, we can try to frame a reflection on our life in other ways. I suggest we pay attention to the feelings that a question or situation evokes. Then we could communally explore the "whys" of that feeling in a contemplative spirit that allows us to really listen to one another. This is different from taking a topic and having a discussion about it. I am talking about taking a topic and cultivating a way of talking and listening to one another. From this kind of exchange can come breakthrough moments when people learn from one another and see possibilities in new ways.

Does this mean that we come to a resolution of action? Possibly. I think what is more important is that this kind of process releases feelings in us so that we are not approaching subjects only in an intellectual way. The Spirit may work through our intellects, but it also stirs in our emotions. If we could explore some of the places and situations where we as women religious experience tension these days in this manner, it could be very helpful. Taking sides and engaging in debates about some of the questions before us is not the way to bring about resolution.

You have talked about how this approach to life can unleash a potential within us to think more creatively. Have you seen this happen?

Yes. I have watched leaders look contemplatively at very difficult situations and come to a decision that they will no longer continue to put energy into a situation that draws them into great negativity. People have become freed to move into a different place regarding situations that have angered them. I saw someone who was being eaten away by her feelings toward a person who had come in and destroyed a program that her congregation had operated for twenty-three years. Through a contemplative approach to this situation, she was freed of the animosity she carried toward that person and could begin again to be creative. It is an internal shift that then affects every external situation in which we find ourselves.

Is there anything that you could recommend to leaders who might want to engage in this kind of approach communally with their congregations?

I think we have to create an atmosphere where we encourage people to take the time for contemplation. Each time we set an agenda for a congregational meeting, we could build in time to pause, be quiet, and not rush to the microphone. We can be intentional in how we structure meetings, in how we invite people into a conversation. The biggest factor, I think, is to give ourselves permission to do this.

More and more people are using the word "contemplation," but I want to stress that it is more than just sitting quietly. The danger there is that we can stay in our heads and think. Contemplation involves getting in touch with the Spirit within, and that takes some discipline. I don't want to minimize what people do, but I get concerned about using a term so much that it begins to mean nothing.

I would recommend that a leadership team start with themselves before they ever bring it to a whole congregation. Does the team embrace a contemplative approach as the way by which it does business? Do the team members allow a synergy to happen when they empty themselves and listen to one another carefully? Teams might say, "But we have two full-time councilors and four part-time, and we come together for only three days a month and we have all this business." These are our realities. However, if we start our meetings with time for contemplative silence and create an atmosphere of real listening, we will have quality conversations and the rest of the business will come more easily. We can enter into the discussions of business items freed of some of the negative thinking that often accompanies our interactions.

You noted that one of the constants in the lives of women religious is that we have always been women of prayer. Would you say more about the power of prayer to effect change?

I believe we are going back to some of the ancient teachings and insights and wedding them with what we are now hearing from science and finding that there is some compatibility. The Institute for Noetic Sciences is one example of an organization that is dedicated to advancing the science of consciousness to serve transformation. It is exploring the effect prayer has on a person even at a distance, and this is rooted in the notion from physics about non-locality, or the direct influence of one object on another, distant object. That seems to underscore the importance and effectiveness of prayer.

Another area where science offers a new interpretation of a traditional concept is that of the communion of saints. We are learning that all reality is interconnected and that all beings have come from the same stardust. I think this makes our communion of saints come alive in new ways. The complement of science and faith helps us to understand in a new way what we knew in our gut, that we could pray and something could happen. How do we let these new understandings come into our conversation and thinking? How do we explore them together?

Given the kinds of situations and places where women religious leaders today find themselves, what advice can you offer for how they can raise up the spiritual dimension of life more clearly?

I think that we can bring the faith dimension into our interactions in a much more explicit way. I find that it's helpful if we can get people to talk about what they are passionate about. You may be in a finance meeting, but can you talk about issues that are larger than money?

For example, I chair my congregation's responsible investment committee. We have high-level talks with people from Detroit Edison on emissions and nuclear power. When a meeting with them is held at our motherhouse, we take the lead at the meeting. The last two times we met we used a reflection piece that helped us share on some common ground before we launched into the issues under discussion. One time we wanted to acknowledge that all of us around the table were doing work that we care about. We spent close to thirty minutes discussing what gives each of us energy in our work, no matter which part of the industry we are involved with. Each of us, whether we were the CEO, the shareholder or consumer, or the legislative advocacy head, spoke. It was very interesting because it shifted our relationship with one another and created a different atmosphere in which we could talk.

The next time we met we shared a reading that encouraged us to consider how things would be if we were to do our jobs in light of their effects on people born two hundred years from now. What would we do differently if our decisions regarding outcomes were not based on quarterly profits, or a two-year election cycle, or the immediate need of a consumer? It was from there that we began our dialogue about alternative energy and nuclear power plants.

Now, can I say that this changed any policies? I can't. But can I say that we all thought about things in different ways after that discussion? I think so. And the people from Detroit Edison keep coming back to talk with us.

I think our emphasis has to be on creating an atmosphere for reflection on the larger questions in ways that don't foster more division among us. As women religious we interact with some of the wealthiest people and some of the poorest, some of the most racist persons and some of the most tolerant, some of the most fundamentalist people and some of the most progressive. How can we work to bridge the chasms? Can we make some difference in a world of such divisions, rather than choose not to speak about the differences as we sometimes do? Can we say, "Let's look at the greater good and what we can foster together"?

When we can keep going to our deepest core with all its passion, that perspective changes our priorities. It changes our behaviors. It changes our beliefs. A contemplative approach to life is a way of being, and if we embrace it, it can change everything.

4

Fostering and Nurturing an Interior Life

Donald Goergen, OP

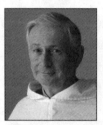 **Donald Goergen, OP**, *is a Dominican priest, teacher, and author. He was previously the provincial for the Central Province of Dominican Friars. Afterward he co-founded a contemplative Dominican community of men and women in which he lived for nine years. He has given retreats in Asia and Africa as well as throughout North America. He currently teaches at the Aquinas Institute of Theology in St. Louis, where he is also the prior of the friars' formation community. He has published many books and articles on religious life, spirituality, and Christology.*

Given Fr. Goergen's dedication to the contemplative dimension of life, LCWR believed his insights on the interior life would be invaluable to those serving in leadership today. In this interview, we explore what it means to be contemplative in a highly frenetic world, how to draw upon the presence of the Spirit, and how exploration of some of the major theological and spiritual questions confronting us today can effectively shape our lives for these times.

There is a strong hunger within religious these days to find ways to live fully inserted into the joys and pain of the world from a deep and grounded contemplative place. What advice could you offer us for how to do this? What does such a life look like? How is it reached?

I think this is an extremely important topic. I was provincial for nine years, and when I finished, I felt that what our province most needed was to retrieve and reown the contemplative dimension of our Dominican lives. Many of my brothers have probably not thought of themselves as contemplatives. We tend to divide religious life into those who are contemplative and those who are active, and most of us see ourselves as active religious. I feel that was a mistake. For us as Dominicans, and this would be true for many other orders, there was a strong contemplative dimension in our history. So how do we retrieve and rediscover this—which isn't easy in a busy, modern, technological world that is focused on efficiency and speed.

After being a provincial I spent two months in India, where I picked up from a wise person a saying that has stayed with me: "It doesn't make any difference how fast you're going if you're headed in the wrong direction." Not that I had a sense that we were headed in the wrong direction, but I felt there was something that we were missing.

I think that being contemplative allows us to be instruments of the Holy Spirit. So, when we hear people say that they desire to live more contemplatively, this doesn't mean they want a quiet life or a pain-free life removed from all the tensions and stresses. Living contemplatively means being more deeply grounded in God. It is standing back from the ways in which we serve the world through all the ministries that we do and taking a look at how we let the Spirit breathe and move through us. Of course, this raises the challenging question of how we know that something is of the Spirit, and not just from ourselves.

I think this desire to live more contemplatively is the work of the Spirit for this period. This may not be on target, but I wonder if the diminishment of vocations to religious life has been for the good. If we had now as many vocations as we have had in the past, none of our congregations would be required to stand back and take a look at where we are going. We would probably keep doing the works we do and trying to respond to all the needs out there—and is this really what religious life is meant to be? Diminishment in numbers has required us to become conscious of the fact that the essence of religious life is less about what we do than about who we are. What does it mean to be contemplative in a very frenetic world?

The question of what religious life can be as we go into the future is a critical one for all in religious life. What other insights on the essence of this life would you like to offer?

It seems that we want to give priority to certain values that have been traditional and maybe need to be rediscovered in a new way, values such as the role of silence in our lives, the time given to prayer, the exploration of forms of prayer that are more meditative or contemplative, being open to making space and taking time to listen to guidance from the Holy Spirit. Someone once wisely said, "Move at the pace of guidance," and I add, "—the pace of the guidance of the Holy Spirit." I think we are almost hardwired to want what we now desire, such as the discipline of giving things time in order to see more clearly or deeply. So much has to do with the busy dimension of our lives and wanting to respond to the tremendous needs of the world out of a certain depth. To do this, we need to take care of our interior lives. So, while I know religious take time for retreats, our religious congregations are structured with so many commitments that it is difficult to allow ourselves time before we reach retirement to explore the interior life. A self-discipline is required to retrieve this asset that I think we sometimes even run from. Although gratification can often come from our ministries, they can also take us from being what we may most need to be at this moment.

Our consumer society has led us to build our identities around what we have. Even in our religious communities it is amazing that much of our lives can get cluttered with what we have. That leads us to ask: Who am I? How do people perceive me? What amount of energy do I give to spiritual practices? What does it mean to simply offer a holy presence? How do we have our ministry flow more out of a deep level of inner life rather than a frenetic response to the horrendous needs of our world? It's not that I have an answer, but I do think if we stand back and ask the questions, the responses would require some restructuring of how we approach matters and what it means to be a spiritual person in our world today. Religious are associated more by the good works we are doing, the corporal works of mercy. But there is also that other dimension of being grounded in God, being a person who listens to the voice of the Lord, who lets God guide.

I think it will make a difference as communities come together and ask what it means for us to be a contemplative community and then own that identity. We need to ask the questions: What is the need—or the hunger—calling for a response from us at this moment in history? What might we look like in fifty years? It would seem that the answer is not to keep doing the same things we have done, but to take a look at this modern, busy, efficient, consumerist society and ask what it would mean to embody God's presence in the midst of it.

You have written about the danger of having an attitude that "prevents the Holy Spirit from breaking through into our lives, our institutions, our cultures, and our histories." You raise the question, "Are we hardened against the Spirit so that the Spirit is unable to breathe or break through?" What are the signs that this hardness exists? What can we do to soften our personal and institutional hearts so that they stay penetrable?

It is interesting that in the scriptures Saint Paul in his letter to the Ephesians says, "Do not grieve the Holy Spirit," and in his letter to the Thessalonians says, "Do not suffocate or extinguish or quench the Holy Spirit." He is quite aware that it is possible for us not to give the Holy Spirit breathing room. Is it possible for us to be so interiorly, spiritually desensitized that the Holy Spirit doesn't have that much space? We need to ask ourselves: In the course of my personal life, what space do I give to the Holy Spirit? Where do we, as religious, suffocate the Holy Spirit? Where today has the church institutionally grieved the Holy Spirit?

We can get caught up—for very good reasons—in our own agendas, our own theologies, and our own deepest convictions that we have formed through experience over decades. But how can we still remain so malleable or flexible to hear the Holy Spirit say that there is something new happening? Whether we are progressive or conservative—and I don't think that language really works for us anymore—we can get so tied into that which gives us an identity and a meaning in life that, while the Holy Spirit can still use us, it may not be as fully or as totally.

I think we have to realize that diversity is a gift of the Holy Spirit as well—and that includes theological diversity. We might not always recognize that as a gift institutionally in the church, and it is easy for us to say when we think another person should think as we do. Karl Rahner, in response to a question he was asked, said that some persons in the church may be given the charism to be an accelerator, while others may be given the charism to be a brake. It can be hard for those who are the accelerators to see what value there is in a brake, and vice versa. So the challenge is to open ourselves more and more to the different calls in the life of the church. Hardness enters in when we discover bitterness or divisiveness or a kind of enduring anger that we cannot heal. Those are the things that, from wherever or whomever they come, are not of the Holy Spirit.

The challenge today is to live a life of integrity in a world with many different voices in it and not let our hearts become hardened through the wounds that we are bound to experience. We need to keep asking ourselves: Am I really open to the ways in which the Holy Spirit might be speaking to the church? We need to do a deep asking of that question on the ecclesial level, as well as on the congregational and personal levels, and not let our thinking become solidified or let our progressive or conservative perspective predetermine how we are going to hear what the Spirit might be saying. This is difficult to do, but I think if we are at least asking the question and living the question in a contemplative way, it may keep us open.

Sometimes what may have been of the Spirit in the past is not necessarily what may be of the Spirit for the church today. We can harden ourselves at times with very good values that can also make it difficult to see what might be coming from elsewhere from a different theological perspective. We can also either canonize or demonize some people. There are people we want to listen to exclusively, or people we don't want to hear from at all. When we do this we put ourselves in a risky position, since we may become less able to hear what the Holy Spirit might actually be saying.

You speak of the Spirit's helping to structure the church and note that the church is a complex system that requires a balance between order and disorder, structure and adaptability. You also note that "the church as structured is always inadequate to the gospel. There is always 'more' to the gospel than the church can express." How can the church best keep the balance needed? What should be the role of its leadership and the role of its membership in keeping the balance?

First, I would like to define the church as a sphere of influence of the Holy Spirit. Irenaeus, the great second-century theologian, once said, "Where the Spirit is, there is the church; and where the church is, there is the Spirit." It is important to keep this link. When we come at the church with anger or negativity or we look at the things of the church that have caused us pain, we are looking at the church institutionally, in its visible form. We need to come at the church with a sense that this is the realm within which the Holy Spirit is at work.

We also have to remember that there is a lot of church outside the visible church, and there is a lot in the church that is not truly the church.

The challenge comes down to seeing these two sides of the church. There is the more charismatic side of the church that Paul speaks of when he writes to the Corinthians about the many gifts, the many ministries, the many ways in which the Spirit is manifest among us—all given to us in diverse ways for the common good. There is also the institutional side. So the question is how to hold these two sides together and in balance. There has to be structure, but that structure has to be very flexible and adaptable over time in order to survive. There has to be order, but that order can never be so rigid that it is no longer alive.

Now we all have our ideas about how to hold the church together. There are those in the church today who are extensively anti-hierarchical, rather than recognizing that there is hierarchy in nature, in life, in institutions. On the other hand, you can go to the other extreme and not be aware of how structure needs to respond to the needs of the time, to feedback from the people, how the Spirit is speaking, or what is happening within the episcopacy. I think that in religious life we have found a way to balance this structurally through our government structures, particularly through our chapters. In chapters, the people have a voice. We elect people to leadership and then the leadership needs to be empowered to lead. How is this possible in the larger church?

I don't expect the church to become democratic, and I think sometimes we idolize democracy in this country. It is by no means a perfect form of government. But I do think that the national episcopal conferences could be strengthened and empowered. I think a mistake made under Pope John Paul II was the great centralization of the church, with less authority given regionally. Do even synods of bishops have some voice—and granted these are still synods of all male bishops—or in the end is it the Holy Father who gathers all the insights and puts out an apostolic exhortation? What a difference it could make if the college of cardinals were more collegial, if it were really a gathering of church leadership from all over the world, with no one group having more influence than others? These are just ways in which we might think about how the leadership could open itself to flexible structures. Structure is valuable as long as the ability to adapt is also there.

We also have to ask what the role of membership is. It is not simply to be servile, but rather to raise questions, to see that the voice of the members is heard, to assure that if there are national episcopal conferences there are opportunities to hear the voices of the people at local levels. So, there may not be a need in the church to give every member of the church a vote, or to have everyone in a diocese choosing the bishop, but there are ways of assuring that people's voices are heard. One of the ways in which the Spirit speaks is through members. As members of a religious community, we also have to ask what our obligations are. We have an obligation to speak and to listen and it is important to ask: To whom do I listen? With whom do I interact? How wide is the circle of voices that I hear? Do I listen mostly to those who think like myself? To what degree is my voice out there in some way?

Drawing on Teilhard de Chardin's work, you note that "the universe is not a cosmos, but a cosmogenesis. It is in the process of coming to be, not yet finished." You go on to say, "God created the world evolutively," and that "evolution is simply God's way of creating the universe." How does this concept influence your own thinking about some of the major questions of these times? Does it help you take a long view on matters and, if so, how?

I think that the thought of Teilhard de Chardin has a great contribution to make. Now this is not to the exclusion of the hundreds of profound voices from the past. In many ways, similar points have been made but without the framework of evolutionary thinking, whereas Teilhard brings that thinking into

touch with a lot of the currents in our world. Teilhard struggled as a scientist and as a priest with this question of evolution as far back as the 1920s when the church wasn't able to
really cope with the implications. He did not see evolution
and creation in conflict with each other. If we look at the universe from the perspective of without—or scientifically, em-
pirically—we see that the universe is evolving. Something
comes to be by way of birth from what was there before. This
does not mean that the universe is not being creative, but
rather that it is being created. If we look at it from the perspective of within—or interiorly—we see the universe being created evolutively by God. So we are saying that God is creating
the universe, and doing so in time, evolutively—or, in other
words, evolution is God's way of creating. Creation isn't instantaneous and it didn't proceed as described in Genesis in
seven days, unless we think of "days" as certain time periods.

Teilhard's contribution was to help us think in terms of
both/and. I think there is an element of both/and in everything. The Gospel of Matthew talks about a scribe who goes
into a storehouse and brings out things that are both old and
new. Which is more important: Love of God or love of neigh-
bor? Adaptability or stability? Inhaling or exhaling? Also,
what may have been required in the past may not be required
now, and what is required now might not be what is required
in forty or fifty or a hundred years from now.

Both/and thinking is not new. Thomas Aquinas structured
his greatest work, the *Summa Theologiæ*, in the same way,
showing that there is truth here and truth there and then having a sense of what lies in the middle. A friend of mine, the
late Dominican priest Ralph Powell, who was a mystic and a
philosopher, said, "It's hard to see the whole picture when you
are inside the frame." It is good to have this perspective—to
remember that we never see the whole picture, but the Holy
Spirit does.

There are implications to seeing things from the perspective of a universe unfolding: the universe is unfinished, the

church is not where it will be, I am unfinished. Teilhard said, "I am a pilgrim of the future on my way back from a journey made entirely in the past." I think his frame of reference helps us to see that what we might want to accomplish in our own day and age may take centuries, especially if we look back historically to the billions of years of life in which species evolved.

I think one of the things that emerged after the Second Vatican Council was a kind of utopian sense, which at the time I thought was good. But by utopianism I mean that somehow we expect the City of God to emerge on Earth in our own lifetimes. We were so imbued with the vision of Vatican II that it was disappointing and difficult to accept that what God was doing might have been different from what we had envisioned, or might be working itself out differently, or might take more time. However, if you had asked a bishop in southern France or a peasant woman in Italy in the year 1000 what the world would be like in the year 2000, they would not have had a clue. Could they have known that there would be scripture in the vernacular, that there was a world outside of Europe, that the Reformation would cause a split in Christianity? If we were to ask ourselves what the church will look like in the year 2500, most of us would say, "I don't care; I want to know what it's going to look like in 2020 when I might still be around." That's the difficulty. On one hand, it is helpful to know that the universe and society and the church are unfinished, but on the other hand it is challenging to realize that there is more that lies ahead than we ourselves might live to see. We can only plant the seeds.

You note that Christians' understanding of Christ is often too small and limited to only Jesus of Nazareth. You explain that the concept of "Christ" refers also to the preincarnate Christ, as well as to the risen Christ and the incomplete Christ. You propose that rather than ponder only the question: "Do I believe in Jesus?" we look as well at the question: "Who is the Christ in whom I believe?" What suggestions could you offer for how we can explore this important question?

I suppose one's faith can be formed at a certain period and then become fossilized, so that how I understood Jesus Christ when I was in fifth grade, or in college, or when I was forty or sixty remains unchanged. If I haven't thought theologically since I was in college, then that is where my faith stays even though my understanding of politics, science, and other disciplines might have been transformed many times. In terms of evolution, we can also see that Christ himself evolves. Note that I am not saying that God is evolving. That is not a concept I would endorse and it is a different matter.

Pope Pius XII in his encyclical on the mystical body said, "Christ requires members." We may not expect that insight to have come from the 1950s, yet it makes sense that if Christ is the head, there can be no head without a body. So if the body of Christ is unfinished, and if we can think of the whole historical, evolving mystical body of Christ, then Christ too is not yet fully formed.

An important question is the one Jesus raises in the Gospels: "Who do you say that I am?" There is the earthly, prophetic, human, divine Jesus of Nazareth, but there is also the Christ. That historical, incarnate embodiment of the Christ is revelatory of whom Christ is. It is not that Christ is something other than that. Christ is that—and more.

In the Pauline vision, the universe itself in its evolution continues to bring something to who Christ is, and it is only in the end that God is in everything and everything is in God. So the question is: How can we keep expanding our consciousness? Teilhard believed that once evolution reached the human sphere it didn't stop, but rather continued as the evolution of consciousness. This is a consciousness that cannot be divorced from the roots from which we come.

This raises a lot of other questions about the value of a particular religious tradition. There are some who think that we will outgrow religion. I am not of that opinion and personally think that most people will come to an awareness of God and have access to the life of the Spirit through their religious tradition. The challenge though will be how religious traditions allow themselves to evolve. So, what might Christianity look like five hundred years from now? How will scripture and the sacraments be made manifest? What will the structures of the church be? Religious traditions need to be open to changes. This doesn't mean that we simply discard the past from which we have come. Just as the Christ is Jesus, full Christianity is holding that revelation that has been entrusted to us while continuing to expand our awareness of what might still lie ahead of us.

5

Living a Discerning Life
in a Complex, Harsh World

Margaret Wheatley

 *Effective leadership requires deep immersion in the pain of the world in which we live and of the people we serve. Doing so can require leaders to fully experience grief, sadness, loneliness, and so many other emotions that many others might choose to avoid. How might leaders develop the skills to dwell healthily with these emotions and the spirituality that will sustain them in these waters?*

*To explore these questions, LCWR turned to **Margaret (Meg) Wheatley**, who has served as an organizational consultant for forty years with leaders on all continents and with most types of organizations and communities. A prolific writer, her articles appear in both professional and popular journals, and her books have included* Leadership and the New Science *(now in eighteen languages) and her most recent work,* So Far From Home: Lost and Found in Our Brave New World. *In this latter work, she invites readers to develop the skills most needed when working for good in this complex and often harsh world.*

In your most recent book, you quote the Buddhist meditation master Chogyam Trungpa as saying, "When tenderness tinged by sadness touches our heart, we know we are in contact with reality. We feel it. That contact is genuine, fresh and quite raw." You go on to say that living from this stance leads to a sadness and loneliness because we see clearly a world that others deny. To live a discerning life, it seems imperative to live from this stance. Would you say more about what it takes to view the world as it is with tender hearts?

What's ironic about this question is that I just completed a long retreat, and this is exactly the question and the practices that my teacher gave me. So that is to say there's no simple answer. But one of the things I am learning is that when we are truly in the tender heart of sadness, we don't feel pride, or arrogance, or any of the nastier ego feelings. We don't feel that we know what's right. What I am encountering in my own practice is what my teacher calls the genuine heart of sadness or the pure heart of sadness—which is actually a very welcoming place. Being there doesn't mean that we try to move out of that sadness and fix the other person for whom we feel the sadness. How to be there is something I have learned from women religious throughout the years. You are fully present to what is going on in the world. Yes, being fully present makes us feel very sad, but it also conditions our hearts so that we feel spontaneous compassion and love. This is a much healthier place to be than a place where you react or get angry or just want to fix a problem that is not solvable. I am finding that feeling a pure heart of sadness is actually a peaceful emotion.

The loneliness is also something that becomes a genuine feeling, but not anything you have to fix. I think what is basic to all of this is the question: How can we just be with our hearts wide open and experience all the depth of that emotion without needing to react? Our tendency when we feel lonely is to react, to try and get over the loneliness, and push away the sadness.

What do you think keeps most of us away from even entering into that kind of a space?

I think we live in a culture that tells us that loneliness is not acceptable—that you don't have to feel lonely, that sadness comes from failure in the pursuit of a happiness which we are so bizarrely focused on. We don't want to feel sad, we're afraid of these things, and yet they're just part of the human experience.

It is impossible to be with the people whom I am with who suffer greatly and experience horrific oppression—and the people whom so many sisters are with—without letting our hearts open to their circumstances. When we do, we feel sadness and perhaps loneliness, although I find loneliness is less of an issue. When I am really standing with others, I don't experience feeling lonely at all.

I would ask the sisters to consult their own experience and what they have discovered in bearing witness or standing with others, because I think we are describing the exact same thing. The key is a commitment to wanting to keep our hearts open.

You also note that we often do not know what to do with our sadness and our grief over the world. You obviously have opened yourself to feeling these emotions quite profoundly. What do you do with your own sadness and grief?

There are basically two things that any one of us does in the face of our sadness and grief. We can shut down and pretend we are not feeling what we are feeling. This, of course, eats away at us over time, and we end up living very distracted lives that are more and more superficial. Our other choice is we can open. Those are the two basic gestures: stand back or move into.

Sadness and grief are a part of my life now, and I actually take that as a good sign. It means that I haven't closed down and that I am on the right path. Keeping my heart open is an important goal of mine. Feeling sadness or grief is a sign that I am doing so.

I want to emphasize one thing though. We have to let these emotions move through us and not let them fester. I recently had a friend who had never smoked die of lung cancer. She told me that lung cancer is on the rise with women and that it is often associated with grief. She was someone who experienced the grief of the world. So what I have learned from her sad death is that it is really important to let the sadness move through us and not hold it in. I think we do that through things like ritual, through singing together, and through liturgy—and it is increasingly important that we do these things. The other side of grief and sadness is joy, so it is important to let the grief mutate into inexplicable joy.

You observe that no one is able to develop insight and compassion without a regular practice of quieting and watching the mind, a practice of some form of mindfulness. Would you talk about your own practice and what it has meant for your own life?

My own practice gets more and more serious as the world gets more and more insane. I could draw a direct relationship between my increased practice and the increase in brutality, disrespect, and anti-human behaviors going on in this country and all over the world. These anti-human behaviors are completely irrational from a human survival point of view, and the more I experience them, the more I deepen my commitment to want to be there for people. I don't want to be one who withdraws. Yet it takes more practice and a stable mind to be able to stay.

I see so much dehumanization going on with policies, programs, and withdrawal of funding decisions that are taking away the social safety net in many countries now. The more I see that, the more I know I want to be of comfort and support to the people who are working in organizations that are trying to assist others. Doing so is a commitment I made many years ago. As I live this commitment, in order to not just lose my temper, become enraged, or be brought down by despair, I need to have a regular daily practice.

My practice is quite modest. I meditate anywhere between fifteen and forty-five minutes a day—depending on my schedule.

I try to keep my awareness very active during the day. What has really developed my capacity, though, is that I go on a solo meditation retreat for two months every winter. My teacher is nearby, and she is a beautiful guide into the depths and heights of spiritual experience. I just completed my fourth such retreat.

What's that retreat like for you, and how do you spend that time?

Well, I'm self-sufficient. I have a beautiful little cabin in the woods up on the tip of Nova Scotia. It is on the sea and it is very wild country—wild weather, wild animals, and a whole monastic community living just a hundred yards from me. I am on my own, and I don't talk to anyone except my teacher or in an emergency situation. I have no Internet, no phone, no computer. What I love most is what happens as I watch my mind come alive when it's free from distraction. And I know we all could have this experience if our lives were not so distracted. On retreat, it is just me and my mind and the books I bring to study. I don't write—and that is a deliberate practice, because writing solidifies your experience into a solid story line rather than keeping your experiences fluid and changing. It is a perfect environment to study pretty obtuse sacred texts. Those texts become so easy to understand in my little cabin, but then I come back here and the text doesn't have much meaning any more other than I vaguely remember it. So one of the things I have observed in doing this regularly is that we are losing our great human mind capacities of memory, connecting the dots, seeing the big picture, thinking ahead, thinking in systems, and seeing interrelationships because we are so distracted and busy with minor disconnected tasks. This has given me insight into the costs of our distracted society, and it is a deep, deep concern to me. We need to reclaim or reawaken our minds through finding undistracted time when we can settle down and reflect.

What would you recommend for those of us who wouldn't be able to make an extensive yearly retreat?

I think taking a day a month or even a half-day dedicated to contemplation or prayer would be very beneficial, as well as going to a weekend or week-long retreat. The main thing here is just to get silent with your mind so that you can see things clearly, which you cannot do day-to-day. It is a complete blessing in my life that I can take this extended time, and because I can, it increases my sense of obligation to be available to people and be in a place of peace instead of a place of rage.

You put yourself in very difficult situations all around the world. What keeps you motivated? How do you keep going?

Well, I never felt I had a choice. When you find your right work, it is the ultimate motivation. I can't think of doing anything else. I also feel I have it pretty easy at this point in my life. I go to where I am invited and get welcomed in by people who are simply happy that I show up for them. I have formed some beautiful relationships through this work. This is a change from my earlier years where my focus was on trying to get people to see from a different worldview.

I live a vowed life, and my vow in Tibetan Buddhism is to achieve an awakened heart and awakened action. Because we believe that we come back after death, my vow is not just for this life. I know I am going to come back, and I just hope that I come back with a more enlightened mind and less ego.

You mentioned the more difficult years of trying to help others to see from another worldview. How do you account for how your ideas have gained so much attention in the more recent years?

Age—and the times! When I was speaking of chaos twenty years ago, people thought it was an interesting concept but that it didn't really apply to their lives. Now everyone is speaking of turbulence and chaos. What is interesting is that I have shifted from thinking that we can fix or change large systems. My work now has shifted away from trying to fix systems and is completely focused on individuals and how we can prepare ourselves to be warriors for the human spirit. It is a significant shift, and the change was motivated by my experience. I don't see our large systems changing, and I am quite concerned that we be prepared for life getting darker and more difficult for many more people. So, this is now my focus. The world is changing, and I have tried to stay in touch with the major changes. I think the skill with which I come to these times is that I can spot trends, and I have been blessed to have a wonderful platform on which to share what I see.

One challenge so many of us face is how to draw out wisdom from all the data and information that comes our way. And a task of leaders is to not only draw out the wisdom but also to articulate its relevance for others. What insights might you share with women religious leaders who are attempting to do this in these complex times?

I am glad you asked this question because I learned something about this by watching the Sisters of St. Joseph as they prepared for the apostolic visitation. In the beginning, there was no agreement among them on how to work with this process. But then, at a large federation gathering, someone named what they perceived to be the true dynamic that had spawned the visitation. From what the sisters told me, once the leaders were able both to name and agree that it was this dynamic— and even though the dynamic was an especially painful one to recognize—once everyone accepted this, they trusted each of the communities to handle the visitation appropriately. Instead of trying to come up with one fixed way to deal with the visitation, they trusted one another to discern how they wanted to respond; the communities did not have to choose the same response. They believed that once the leader had identified what was really going on, then they could trust the members to respond appropriately.

What I take from that, and what I have seen in secular settings as well, is that there is a real need for leaders to name what is going on in a situation, and to name it truthfully, and then let that truth be what people talk through. Once a group has a common definition of what is going on, then the group can be free to self-organize, and there is no need for rules about how to respond. Then people can trust one another more. If, however, we are all operating from a different storyline on what the situation is, it only creates confusion. Then people do not act in accordance with one another.

I see this in my own work. Once we agree on what is going on, we trust one another to self-organize appropriate responses. But if we have competing stories about what is happening, then your behavior is going to be very different than mine.

Another crucial role for leaders is to recognize that they're the only ones who see the whole and its patterns. Leaders need to be "stewards of the whole" organization. No one else is even interested in seeing what is happening elsewhere because we are all so overworked and busy. So it is the leader who periodically must stand back—hopefully with a group of others—and look at the patterns, look at what is happening, and name it for others. This is the only way we can stop going down this path of blind action that doesn't lead us to anywhere good. So, it is really not about data; it's about seeing patterns and naming them correctly.

I have seen sisters able to take negative things they have experienced and view them as part of a larger pattern of oppression of women. Seeing from this perspective helps us find much more meaning in the particular negative experience in which we find ourselves, and rouses our courage to name it for what it is.

Women religious are dedicated to bringing religious life forward in a form that meets the current needs of the world and anticipates how it might meet the needs of the future. You have noted that thinking forward is impossible for people fearfully reacting to the present moment. Would you say more about how fear prevents us from thinking forward and hinders our ability to discern wise action for the future?

I want to first say something about fear. There is a wonderful quote by the Persian writer Hafiz who said, "Fear is the cheapest room in the house. I would like to see you living in better conditions." Fear is the simplest place to occupy, and what is so bizarre about fear is that it is never found in the present moment. The paradox here is if we want to think forward we cannot do it from a position of fear, yet all our fear comes from thinking about the future. Fear comes from how we interpret the past and how we worry about what will happen in the future.

The first requirement for thinking forward free from fear is to be fully present in this moment, as well as open to all the information that is out there. Fear gives us such terrible lenses through which to view the future; it can become quite terrifying. When I find myself in fear, I try to come back to the present moment and what is going on right here, right now. What do I have? Who am I? Who is around me? I work at trying to prevent my mind from going into some future fear-filled state. This also works when we are trying to develop a strategy for the future or think about who we want to be in the future. First, we have to take full stock of what we have right now. This gives us a really amazing capacity then to think forward.

Fear has also become a deliberate political strategy. We are told that we have a lot of enemies and are presented with a lot of fearful prospects for the future. What is interesting is that some of those fearful prospects are true, such as those having to do with climate change. But when we are presented with those facts in the context of fear, we tend to say, "Well, we can't do anything about this anyway, so let's just lead a great life while we can."

What has drawn you to working with women religious? Is there a potential you see in women religious that we should perhaps attend to more?

For a number of years I had been speaking about organizations that take all their direction from their strong sense of values. In 1992, one of my colleagues told me that if I was going to continue talking about such organizations, I should be working with two groups: the military and women religious. I have worked with both, and he was right. Both of these groups are comprised of people who have a strong sense of commitment to their values and, of course, very different means to achieve ends.

As I got to know sisters, I found they were the strongest can-do leaders on the planet. I came up with a slogan years ago, which was: If you want it done, ask a nun. Sisters never seem to say no, you all seem to just make it work. I have loved that. I also love the focus on charism, as well as ritual and liturgy. You have the means to create a strong container to hold your separate activities and work in the world. I loved learning what it means to bear witness and to stand with. All of this was so new to me at the time I first met sisters, but now it is just a part of who I am. I also love the fact that sisters pray for me, and I really feel those prayers.

Another valuable lesson I have learned from you is how to create community. A number of years ago I was physically and emotionally exhausted and went on my first-ever spiritual retreat (in a Benedictine community). While on the retreat I met a sister who knew of my work. I was telling her how much I was out in the world working, traveling a great deal, moving from place to place. She just looked at me and said: "You need a community!" It was like a mother saying to a child: "You need to put on a coat—it's cold out there." That understanding of community has really attracted me. One of the greatest needs we all have is to come back together and support one another in a very difficult time.

Several years ago, I joined with a group of sisters and lay women (we called ourselves "The Willing Disturbers") to explore this question: "What might be the next form of consecrated life for women who don't want to be nuns, but whose work is sacred?" I love this question because it points to community. This question just keeps growing bigger and bigger in my own mind and in the minds of my colleagues. How do we want to be together, to support one another, and also help one another do great work in the world? This is a question that is percolating in a lot of places, and it isn't just focused on women religious. It's a question for me personally. I have a large family, so I feel I have support. But it is critical to also find a community where I would feel supported spiritually.

From all the work you have done with women religious and all the potential you see, are there any liabilities you have observed that may also hold us back?

I would say a liability is believing the negative messages about yourselves that are directed to you. My observation is that those messages do not come from those you serve, but from elsewhere. My suggestion is that you look at the source of the negative messages before you accept and give attention to them. It's not easy to avoid internalizing the negative, but I think we do that by observing from where it comes.

There is a great quote from Buddha who said nearly twenty-six hundred years ago: "They criticize the silent ones; they criticize the talkative ones. There is no one in the world who escapes criticism." As women stand up more and more in settings all around the world, we are getting more and more criticism. This is part of the last stages of desperation in any organization or culture. We strike out at one another, seeking to blame the others rather than examine ourselves. It is part of the times in which we live.

Do you have suggestions for what women religious leaders can do to be the effective leaders for which these times call?

Fully acknowledge that you are effective leaders for these times. But remember that this strength and confidence can only come from within. Don't wait for or expect it to come from other sources. I encourage you to understand the power of your charism. Understand the incredible stories of your founders. People who persevere usually come from strong lineages—and you have that.

This is a crazy and very anti-human time. Therefore your work—and my work—is rising in importance. Have the strength and the confidence to do it and continue to find ways for all of us to support one another in it. And realize that our faith in people, and in the sacred, must always be attended to as our ultimate source of motivation and strength.

LEADERSHIP
AND PROPHETIC IMAGINATION

6

The Power and Potential
of Prophetic Communities

Joan Chittister, OSB

 *International lecturer, author, and advocate for peace **Joan Chittister, OSB**, addressed the 2006 LCWR assembly on the future of religious life. The former LCWR president challenged women religious to fully live their call to be prophetic. She emphasized, however, the power and potential of not just prophetic individuals, but more so, prophetic groups. In this interview, LCWR probed the question of how a leader can inspire a group to claim its power as an agent of change and transformation in the world.*

Would you talk about the difference between a prophetic person and a prophetic congregation?

The prophetic congregation is a congregation that "as a congregation" stands for something. For example, there is hardly anybody who does not know that the Sisters of Mercy stand in support of women. They have a particular focus and it is that focus of the congregation as a whole that enables the congregation to speak with a prophetic voice. If you have a hundred people and one of them is concerned about women's issues, that's one thing and it's a good thing. And the other ninety-nine are probably concerned with ninety-nine other issues and those are good things, too. But, if you want the congregation itself to have ultimate impact, the members have to know how they are practicing their charism as a group.

The stunning part of this is that it is not new. This is how we were all founded. If you look at any congregation's history, you will get to the sentence that says, "The sisters of such-and-such were founded to..." That was the prophetic role that they took at that time. We stood for the education of Catholic children in a white, Anglo-Saxon, Protestant society. We stood for the care of Catholic immigrants in a society that did not want Catholic immigrants. That was our prophetic posture 150 years ago. Now, thank God, it ceased to be prophetic someplace along the way. It isn't that we failed; it is that we succeeded.

So what is the difference today? We are into very different dimensions of social pressures now, and they come at various and multiple levels. Yes, of course, you can go on teaching, but for what purpose? What is your prophetic message for the rest of the world? If your prophetic message is that we cannot abandon single mothers and fatherless children, then this can be done in all sorts of ways. We can advocate for legislation that gives workers a decent wage. We can set up pastoral centers that we oversee, if not staff. We can go into the slums and the boroughs and the housing projects and the urban centers and have evening courses to teach single parents how to budget, how to bathe their babies, what food to buy, how to set up a crib. We can send people to Washington to pressure for legislation to make it possible for a poor family to not just exist, but to have a decent standard of living. We can help the poor family in our own backyard. We can go in their backyards and live with them there. But we do all of that knowing that when we are doing it, we are doing it to advance this issue, to magnify this message. The prophetic congregation magnifies a clear, single message.

How do you think this prophetic role will assist in the process of transforming religious life? How could not fully engaging this dimension influence the future of religious life?

The church itself calls religious life the prophetic dimension of the church. The church has an expectation of us. What does the prophet do? The prophet doesn't foretell the future. The prophet simply says the truth in an environment where the truth is not being heard, is not welcome, is being resisted, and is unacceptable. A prophet says: "See what's in front of you. Don't tell me that the economy is better this year. The economy is better for you. But you're not seeing the effects; you're not looking. You don't care about the effects on everybody else, on these people, on this part of society, in this part of town, for these children, for this kind of person." The prophet is a truth-teller who speaks from the center of the society. What truth is your congregation telling you? What truth do you as a congregation tell now?

What is the effect of that on the future of religious life? It's easy. If we stop being the prophetic dimension of the church of the people of God, if we stop being the truth-tellers that the people of God can count on, then why should we exist?

As leaders are working toward the transformation of their own congregations, what are some of the concrete things that you think they could do?

First, there is a question missing in this interview and that is: What is the role of the leader? Sisters can't sit down together at breakfast in the morning and intuit what the message of the congregation is. The congregation has to arrive at that message together/purposely, own that message, and then, on an individual basis, take it to where they are. Now, they can't own that message as a congregation unless the leader believes it. My own feeling is that there is not enough of this happening. In a period of dire crisis, transition, pressure—use whatever euphemism you want—there is a great temptation to stress what is safe. Prayer is safe, community is safe, responsibility in the ministry is safe. What is not safe is to define the truth and figure out how this congregation is going to tell it. You can't do this without leadership. If this doesn't happen, it's because leadership doesn't enable it to happen. I am not saying that leadership makes this happen, forces this to happen, imposes this so it does happen. I am saying that leadership must create the process and maintain the process that leads the community deeper and deeper and deeper as a community into the message that it intends to tell as a community.

The message of a prophetic congregation must be a conscious articulation of the truth that this culture needs at this time, on this issue. If the leader isn't leading that, how can we be surprised that the congregation seems to be going nowhere at all?

Do you think there is a reticence among leaders to lead in that way?

Yes. It isn't that leaders don't want to do this, but they are feeling very burdened by the exigencies of this moment, such as aging members and declining membership. Leaders are saying, "How can we talk about the war in Iraq? We're so busy doing the dishes, enlarging the infirmary, getting the office book reprinted." Well, get un-busy about those things. Get busy about what we need to be busy about. Put your money there, put your time there, and put your community meetings there.

The other thing is that this is dangerous. If you are really speaking to the society in which you live, and it's with a message that this society needs to hear, a lot of people are not going to like you saying it—at least at first. You can't call yourself a prophetic congregation and not walk in the footsteps of Jesus and the prophets. So, this is truth time. We have to ask: Are we telling ourselves the truth about who we are, what we do, and why we're here? Maybe we are not. Maybe that is why disappearance is so likely. Or, maybe we are being trimmed down to travel lightly.

We finished the last era, and we did it very well. Now the question is: Are we going to walk into this one? Or, are we going to just say, "Whoa, that's for the next generation,"—if there is a next generation—and go quietly and silently away? Mary Luke Tobin didn't go quietly and silently away. After I gave my presentation at the LCWR assembly, Mary Catherine Rabbitt (president of the Sisters of Loretto) told me that she had visited Mary Luke on her deathbed before coming to the assembly and told her that I was speaking. She asked Mary Luke if there was any message that she wanted her to take to me. Mary Catherine said that Mary Luke raised her fist in the air and said, "Carry on!" She died soon after. Mary Catherine said to me, "When you ended your speech, I was in a state of shock. It was as if Mary Luke had gotten to you before I did. It was as if her last message to us was, 'Carry on!'" That's what it's all about. It doesn't take 125,000 people; it took three when our congregations started. We were doing the right thing then and people recognized it. Women recognized it, the church recognized it, and society recognized it—and hated it. Those first women bore the brunt for us and for the integrity of our congregations. The question is: Will we maintain the integrity at another crossover point in time?

When you think about what religious life might look like once we have "crossed over," do you have any images in your own mind?

I sure do. You have to understand that I come at religious life out of a Benedictine filter, and I know that every community structure has its own character, and must, and should. First, I am convinced that religious life will be small. We are starting over. Until you get that through your head, you can't understand any of the rest of this. Find out who your foundresses were. Know who your first five women were. Know their names and their ages. Memorize them and say them, because that's who you are now. We're starting over.

Second, it must be spiritually intense. What we do, what we think, the message we give must be given by the prayers that we say, the spirituality we bring to everything we do. It will come out of the cry of the psalmist. It will come through the Gospels.

Third, religious life will be clear and easily recognizable because it will be wrapped well around the message. When people see us, they will know what is missing—what is missing in them and what is missing in the world.

Fourth, religious life is going to function as congregations, as groups. People will know that that group does this, that group believes this, that group is about this. Then we won't be worrying about numbers.

If you could give one message to leaders that you most want them to remember these days, what would it be?

That this is no time for despair. This is the moment of the call to begin again. Interestingly enough, in scripture the spiritual call to great things has almost always been to the elderly, the frail, or the resistant. Abraham was not a young man when he was told to start over. Moses spent forty years in the desert and never got to the Promised Land. Ezekiel got his vision while in captivity, when it looked as if the whole place had fallen apart. Joshua began to lose the minute he tried to work in the new land. Even Gideon, the one person in scripture who got himself completely prepared for the struggle, got turned around, and was told to send home three-fourths of the army to fight the battle that God had told him to wage. I swear that this is a Gideon moment. Our army has been sent home. We don't need an army now to do what we're supposed to do.

We cannot despair and we have to stop using the "age card." This is a call. It is not a failure; it is a call. The questions

are: Can we hear it? Will we respond to it? How will we respond to it? Do we get it? Or have we taken the position that
things are clearly over, so let's just live it out? What seeds are
you sowing, because this is a beginning time, a seed-sowing
time? We are the bridge-builders and the transition-makers.
That does not mean that we have the right to sit down and
quit midstream. We are also not defiantly about saving religious life. There are a thousand institutions that could do anything that we have done. We are not here to save religious life.
We're here to do the Gospel—at every stage and age of our
lives, and to do it together.

*You're obviously a person who hasn't given up. What keeps you
going?*

A great sense of humor and a very long view of history that
comes with being a Benedictine. I honestly believe that we
live in the center of the scriptures, that we're still writing
those scriptures, and that we're the characters in those scriptures now. The scriptures are a template of our own lives.
Where do you fit? How do we write our scripture in our time?
None of us is perfect and every one of us has failed. But, what
were you doing when you failed? What were you doing as you
stumbled along? Where were you going? What is important is
not that you are stumbling, but whether you know where you
are going. Do you insist on getting there? Can you get there
without being distracted, without being stopped, without sell-
ing out? I just don't want to go quietly.

*You won't! Are there practices or disciplines in your own life that
you could recommend to leaders to help them keep going?*

I am a social psychologist so I am very interested in groups—
the effect of people on groups and groups on people. Institutional renewal and reorganization have always fascinated me.
So I ask myself consistently: What should we be doing here?

Where do we fit here? What are we seeing here? What are we saying about what we are seeing?

I also play a little piano, I love parties, and I don't take anything so seriously that I don't insist on playing in the middle of it. This apparently has sustained me for a long, long time. I'm not negative, I'm not bitter, and I'm not angry, but I am very clear about what I myself see, and I am trying to raise questions. I am not saying that I know all the answers, but I do know the questions. I simply refuse to abandon the questions because they are the questions of our time.

How can we say that we are the prophetic dimension of the church and not attend to the questions of our times? All of our congregations started in response to a question of their time. Every congregation should ask itself: What questions were our foundresses trying to answer? Mother McCauley's surely must have been: Why don't they teach the girls to read? Vincent de Paul's questions must have been: Why is no one feeding these children? Why do these people not have clothes? We need to ask: What question confronted our congregation at the time of its beginning? What question does our congregation have about these times now? And, don't tell me that we don't know what to do. Find your question and you will know the answer, and you will know what you should be doing in your area to answer that question. This is not difficult, but it takes real commitment, courage, and the willingness to begin again, and that's what we don't want to do. That's the secret in the system right now: it's comfortable. We're saying, "What is she talking about? We just got it made. I finally got the overstuffed chair that I wanted all my life and now I'm going to sit in it for the rest of my lifetime." Every congregation has to decide for itself how to begin, but it has to begin. If not, we shall find ourselves drowning in worthlessness, useless to everybody and anybody.

Is there anything that you would like to see LCWR do to help religious life at this time?

I did say one thing in the presentation at the assembly that I was really serious about. I think LCWR could facilitate the maximization of religious presence by asking the members: What is the question of this time? In what central way could we answer the question? Would you tithe to help begin the answer to this question? We did it once when we helped start NETWORK. We could keep doing these things, we could do something every year, every three years, every five years, and it would be significant. We could choose a village in Africa and wipe AIDS out of that village. But this takes leadership. We have to have leadership.

We have to decide what extra we will do to make something like this happen. If LCWR took a neighborhood—one neighborhood—and changed it—sent in tutors, worked with Habitat for Humanity, planted flowers and trees, came in with reading programs—every single newspaper in the country would be carrying the story in its headlines. There would be women out there saying, "That's what I have been thinking about doing with my life." And to those who would say, "That's a bit showy, Joan," I would answer, "And so were the first schools you built in every single, small, rural village in this country. And that's where the kids saw goodness, effectiveness, concentration, and life-giving sacrifice on their behalf. This is what we need to do today.

7

Prophetic Imagination: A Call to Leaders

Walter Brueggemann

The Prophetic Imagination *has been one of the most important texts for anyone seeking to understand the prophetic impulse and the potential of alternative communities. The book's author,* **Walter Brueggemann**, *an ordained minister in the United Church of Christ and one of the world's leading Old Testament scholars, applies biblical wisdom to the challenges of contemporary society in a way that illuminates possibilities for deep change in the world's social structures. Because of the critical need for leaders to nurture their own as well as their organizations' imagination and creativity, LCWR interviewed Dr. Brueggemann on his insights about the prophetic imagination and its relation to the challenges facing the world today.*

With our increased access to information, our exposure to global realities, and our capacity to use new technologies, one would think that our facility to imagine would be even stronger. What do you think is happening in general to our capacity to imagine?

I think our capacity to imagine is shrinking. We are becoming kind of one dimensional and not really free or able to risk thinking outside of the box, and that's really sad. The partisan tone that we're getting out of Washington reflects the fact that everything is reduced to party ideology. The whole artistic dimension of the human spirit is largely shriveling among us.

What do you do to keep your own capacity for imagination alive?

I'm not sure I keep it alive so well, but I think I do my best imagining at the tip of my pen, which is why writing is important to me. I'm often surprised when I write because by the time I get to the end of a paragraph I find that what I thought I was going to write in the beginning isn't at all what I ended up with.

I think my endless study of scripture keeps my imagination alive. I also do a lot of other reading. I read some novels and some poetry, but my real interest is in historical biography. I find it opens up new angles of vision and new dimensions of thinking for me. I have to have a lot of input so that I can keep reorganizing my own data around other images and metaphors.

Would you say more about your reading of sacred scripture?

I do basically historical, critical study, and I always do it in the interest of the church. So I am always extrapolating and turning from an exegete into a preacher as I look at scripture in light of what is happening today. So my work is often criticized among scholars for being too contemporary and too pushed toward what it means today, rather than what it anciently meant.

When I work with scripture, I basically think about justice questions. I have come to see that pain really is the interpretive key. The connections I try to make for the sake of the church basically have to do with how the Gospel responds to situations of pain in the world. I believe the cross is the entry point for an interpretive practice of pain because the cross disclosed the profound pain of God. So I am very attracted to feminists, liberationists, and neo- and postcolonial interpretation—all of

which seem to arise out of historical and sociological dimensions of pain. I think I then bring my own sense of the pain
that's around me in the people I know.

There are, of course, many texts of the Bible that aren't directly concerned with pain, but I tend to gravitate to those
that are when I teach in the church. I find those are the texts
that really interest people and the ones that people want to
talk about more.

*What you choose to write about and speak on clearly touches
people's hearts today.*

Well, I think that's true because when the church is faithful to
these particular texts, it becomes for very many people the
only venue where they have the chance to talk about pain.
The rest of the world is too busy and too fast and too self-as-
sured and dares not linger over the reality of suffering and
pain.

*You speak often about "living inside God's imagination." What
does that mean for you?*

In the last five years or so I've been thinking that a lot of the
objectionable texts about God in the Old Testament have to
be taken seriously as revelations of who God was or how God
was, rather than saying they are mistaken human projections
of God—which is something I've thought a lot myself. The
reason for my saying this in response to your question is that it
seems to me that God's imagination is pluralistic and conflicted and disturbed and dynamic and under way.

This is important because my experience of the church
(and when I say that I am not talking about the Roman
Catholic Church, but rather the Protestant traditions, but I
think this applies to churches beyond ours) is that it wants to
flatten out God's imagination and make it a seamless story of
love, mercy, grace, and all the good things. However, I find,

particularly in the prophetic texts, that God was in a lot of conflict over how to relate to Israel through Israel's disobedience and recalcitrance. If that is the correct reading, then I take comfort in knowing that I was made as an image of God because my own imagination is quite conflicted and unsettled and pluralistic.

I think God's imagination, as given to us in scripture, is bent toward healing and transformation and newness, but it's not without conflict.

You also speak often of the call to "set God free" from the captivity caused by our own rules and structures. What suggestions do you have for how we can allow or make space for God to do something uniquely new, something beyond our imaginations, and possibly beyond our inclinations as well?

In Protestantism, Karl Barth was the great interpreter who, one hundred years ago, exploded much of our scholarship by simply asserting out of the book of Romans that God really didn't set our rules or structures, or our propositional theology, or any of our conventional certitudes or conclusions. I think in our conventional interpretation, we always want to shave God down so that God is not an inconvenient truth for us. Of course, when we do that, there isn't any good news because the news always is of God breaking out of our boxes and patterns to create new possibilities for us. On one hand, that is what makes the Old Testament so interesting, because the sky is always so incredibly explosive and unsettling. Serious people are finding those gospel breaks in their own lives, just when they thought that everything was settled and arranged.

Good study and good prayer really are about living with an openness to God's not honoring our predictability and our control. Now, that is not very easy for any of us, because we are so capable of deceiving ourselves and imagining that we are open when we are not. If we think of Isaiah 43, where God says not to remember the former things because "I am doing a new thing," we realize that God is always doing something new and we're always running to catch up with it. It requires a great deal of critical self-awareness to become attentive to, on the one hand, how we tend to shut things down and, on the other hand, how we really do yearn to have things broken open.

My conviction is that people come to church precisely with that ambivalence—that they are scared to death that something is going to happen that is going to explode the way that they have the world arranged. That tends particularly to be the case when anything is mentioned about social questions. At the same time, they have a profound hunger for something that is way beyond the way they produced their life. The pastoral task is to move in precisely on that ambivalence, where we want God to be free for us and where we're scared that God will be free against us.

You note that now is not a time for answers, but for questions that defy answers. How readily do you find that perspective accepted? How do you counter the desire so many people have today for certainty and clear-cut answers?

I do believe this is a time for questions without answers, except that I would want to qualify that by saying that in the biblical faith or gospel faith, there is a certain frame of reference in the big narrative picture so that we are not totally at sea about the kinds of questions we need to be asking. The questions have a certain form and shape because of the historical fabric in which those questions are embedded.

My experience of teaching lay people in the church (and, of course, my experience is highly selective, since I only get invited to certain kinds of churches and certain kinds of venues) is that people are welcoming of a chance to think beyond accepted questions. I think people are exhausted by what they experience as the authoritarianism of the church, where the church is tempted to act as if all the questions are settled. Here

not only don't we have to think any more, we are not permit-
ted to think any more. Marcus Borg, who is a friend of mine,
often tells people that the real claims of the Gospel are very
lean, and the other archaic teachings don't have to be embraced. I think people heave a sigh of relief when they find out
they don't have to carry all these old beliefs. I'm not for scut-
tling the tradition, but much of the tradition has become en-
crusted and frozen—to mix the metaphors—and the way it is
formulated doesn't really minister to people.

My discovery as a teacher is that people have these stereotypes of fundamentalism and of scholasticism, but what they
really want to know is whether you can make sense out of the
biblical or Gospel narratives without falling into those old for-
mulations. I find a lot of people want to rethink all of this—
not because they are renegades or rebels, but because the
Gospel always has to be reformulated to come to terms with
peoples' available experience. I don't think we have done a
very good job of that, and that's what makes being a pastor or
teacher really interesting, productive, and exciting.

*You have suggested that we ask ourselves if we have enough free-
dom to imagine or articulate anything new in the situations in
which we find ourselves. What do you think robs us of the courage
and power needed to think alternative thoughts?*

On one hand, I think it's just our habits. We readily fall back
on what we know and the way we know it. The other factor is
the economic risk that can be involved. We have our anten-
nas out pretty far to recognize the social, economic, and political threats to our own vested interests if we go very far down
the road of biblical testimony.

The truth that has been entrusted to us puts us at risk. The
risk is not just intellectual, meaning I am thinking about what
I never thought about before or didn't know before. The risk is
also an economic one in terms of social power, social privilege,

and social entitlement. Even people who are not theologically very sophisticated can quickly connect the dots when we speak of biblical testimony, and they don't welcome what we are saying. And when pastors and teachers are looking at how to manage their budgets, they often don't want to upset people with wealth and power. I can't tell you how many Protestant ministers have told me in the last couple of years that they don't dare mention in their congregations the war in Iraq. To tell their congregations what they really think about the war could put their whole operation at risk. It's very tricky to find the courage or freedom to speak freely of alternative futures when you are putting your economic base in jeopardy.

You stress the importance of the role of public lament in order to move to a new place. You note that the capacity to admit that things are not right and to grieve that reality is the first step in offering serious criticism. Who do you think needs to hear our lament today?

I think God needs to hear our lament. But I would rather ask the question: Who needs to speak lament today? I think those who need to speak lament are the wounded people—those wounded by exclusion, or brutality, or whatever else.

I think we have to bear in mind that in the United States today increasing numbers of people are becoming more aware that the world we thought we were going to have—which was white and safe and well ordered and prosperous and productive —is gone. I think that's where the adrenaline comes against gays and lesbians, or against healthcare reform. I don't necessarily think the adrenaline is about the issues, but rather it's about an underlying sense of loss that we haven't yet articulated about the world we really wanted slipping through our fingers. So, now we are going to have to get used to a world that is multicultural in more extended ways and that is economically less extravagant.

If this is a correct analysis, then I would say almost everybody in our society needs to be practicing lament, and the people who need to be hearing lament are the people in the power structure—whether that be the power structure of the church, government, corporate society, or wherever. The laments are basically all about the poor distribution of power and wealth and resources for living, and the suffering of some people because others have too much. Laments are basically about the imbalance people experience in their lives. In the ancient psalms of lament people complain about their enemies who tend to be people who have exploited or taken advantage of them. They even lament against God who abandons them and is not faithful.

I think we live in a society of huge loss. I think by its emphasis upon gratitude and grace and good things, the church encourages people to engage in denial of the losses. Lament is a refusal to engage in denial.

Are there other endings that you believe we particularly need to publicly address?

The European enlightenment period, where Western white males (like me) controlled everything and knew everything, is now coming to an end. That touches everything. I don't know what a Roman Catholic would think about the situation of apparent abuse in the Irish Catholic church, but I see it as almost a metaphor for everything in our society that has been arranged from the top down. For example, we have a Congress now that's completely controlled by billionaires who basically vote money for their lobbyists, and on and on. All of this is ending, and it's going to be a long time dying because old power is enormously resistant.

I think people have a sense of an ending occurring. For the many people in our world who have been excluded, this is good news, but, of course, it is bad news for the others. In many sectors of our society, the church provides the only place where we can process this. My experience of the church, though, is that we don't do a very good job of this. We are equipped to do it, and people are ready to have us do it, but we need to find the ways to do it.

Along with public lament over what is being lost, what are some of the hopes and yearnings we all carry within us that need to be brought to public expression as well?

I think we carry within us personally a hope that things are going to be better. It's argued that in the Old Testament laments really are acts of hope. They are not acts of resignation, but they are insistences that things have got to change and can change. The interface of loss and hope is the counterpoint to denial and despair. Our society specializes in denial, and if you break into denial then people plunge into despair. Lament and hope are intrinsic to each other. I suspect that the only people who can honestly lament are those who have some hope that things in the world aren't right and that they don't need to stay this way.

How can we deal with the reality that sometimes we may be serving as the prophetic imagination and at other times we are very much a part of what you call the "royal consciousness"? [Brueggemann uses the term "royal consciousness" to refer to the dominant culture against which the prophets are regularly a counterpoint.]

I think it's a given that any one of us in our social groupings may practice prophetic imagination and also participate in the royal consciousness. The important thing is to maintain some kind of self-awareness and intentionality so we know what we are doing when we are doing it. The problem I have with many liberals is that we imagine we are being prophetic, when, in fact, what we are really doing is fostering our own royal consciousness. So I think that going back to the sources of pain can help us monitor our fostering of any of that.

Do you have any observations to make about how U.S. Catholic women religious are being a prophetic community? Do you have any observations about how we may be missing opportunities to be a prophetic voice?

I used to say if the world is ever saved, it will be saved by English teachers. Now I think if the world is saved, it will be saved by nuns. The courage of Catholic women religious is a model and a source of strength that is indispensable. Obviously it's indispensable for the Catholic Church, but it's also indispensable for society more broadly. No doubt you are missing opportunities; there's more that can be done. But I think communities of Catholic women religious don't know how much the rest of us outside the Catholic Church value and count on your life of testimony. I really want to celebrate that and affirm it all I can.

If U.S. women religious were to become truly prophetic, alternative communities, where do you see that possibly taking us?

I see that taking you into trouble. Nobody has all that down yet, do we? It is such a dangerous time, yet it's also such an important time to have the kind of witness that you all do. I want to accent how important your testimony is to the rest of us, and that needs to be said more than it is. I just marvel at your courage.

LEADING WITH VISION

8

Articulating a Vision for the Future

Nancy Schreck, OSF

*People need strong leaders who articulate a vision for the future that inspires others to live and work with hope and not lose heart in the face of challenges. When leaders communicate the organization's future direction in clear and compelling ways, they provide a focus and energy that engender hope and a sense of purpose.*
*LCWR engaged one of its former presidents, **Nancy Schreck, OSF**, to reflect on this important leadership role. A former leader in her own community of sisters, she has worked nationally and internationally as a presenter and facilitator. She is currently ministering in Okolona, Mississippi.*

You have said that there is something distinctive that religious life has to offer. What would you name as that distinctive quality?

I would name three things. First is an unapologetic loyalty to the needs of people who are poor and marginalized. Each time a new form of religious life has been born, it was in response to a compelling need. That loyalty to new needs is what is core to us. We have also been our best selves in religious life when, once those needs were taken care of, we moved on to the next new need. It is natural that any time something gets institutionalized, it gets a bit stuck. The very best thing that institutions do is to help us meet needs. The danger is that they can become ends in themselves. This is some of the struggle that we are in now.

The second thing is a nuance on the first and that is that our work is not just social work, but rather it is responding to critical needs and doing social critique through the lens of the reign of God, with an unapologetic loyalty to the vision of Jesus. There is a new book, *Great Mystics and Social Justice: Walking on the Two Feet of Love*, that tells the story of how people like Dorothy Day, Gandhi, and Thomas Merton were able to blend the social and mystical tradition together. I think that this is our purpose in religious life: to attend to the mystical and the prophetic, with each feeding the other all the time.

The third thing comes from Paul VI, who said that there should be in religious life a willingness to be at the frontier. Core to religious life is this constant seeking for new ways to apply the Gospel. This is not to say that we are the only ones doing that, but we'd better be doing it.

What role does the communitarian context of religious life play today?

Alice Walker has this wonderful line: "Everything that the world really needs is too big for individuals to give." In these days when many members are in individual ministry, the communitarian witness is both radical and needed. The challenge of those three distinctive qualities is so massive that I don't know how anybody could do it alone. As we find ourselves in the middle of great needs and trying to do social critique, we need one another's perspective, correction, encouragement, and clarification, because the needs in this time are so complex. Maybe in times past we needed big numbers to get the work done. Now I think we need one another so that we can discern together in the midst of the complexity.

You have noted that little has happened since the mid-1990s when religious were told of the fifteen-year window of opportunity for making significant change in our lives. Why do you think this is so?

I think we got into a mode of focusing more energy on our re-linquishment than on our future. We knew that our numbers were changing and we put a lot of things in place to be ready for this. This was good and what was needed. Now I am con-cerned about our lack of imagination and lack of passion to do the things we need to do to ensure a future. I think that most people in religious life, until the last ten years, have taken for granted that there would be a future for religious life. People often say, "We believe we have a future, but we don't know what it will look like." Or "We believe that God will take care of us." This kind of thinking has kept us too vague.

I think we aren't doing the kind of work it takes to imag-ine a future. One of the blocks to this type of work could be the tendency of groups to get into some judgmental behavior, saying, "If only we had done this," or "We never should have done that." This really doesn't help us. What helps is imagin-ing what you want to be like in the future. We seem to be swimming in this sea of a corporate depression about dying, and we don't know how to choose life in the midst of it. It is easy to choose life when it's all positive and there are a hun-dred life choices. But when it looks like death and diminish-ment are staring us in the face, there's a kind of heaviness that blocks our creative imagining for the future.

Do you think there is still time for us to creatively imagine for the future?

Yes, I definitely do! I once heard Rosa Parks speak when she was about seventy-five years old. She said, "As long as I can put one foot in front of the other, I have to be about the work of justice." I use this as a parallel: we don't need to be young, and we don't need to be big. But if we are committed to what religious life is about, then there is a passion for doing what needs to be done to imagine that new kind of future.

You've noted a reticence among some leaders to articulate a vision for religious life and for their congregations. Why do you think this is so?

First of all, articulating a vision takes courage. Unless leaders are really secure that this is their role and are willing to be honest with their members about their vision for religious life, I don't think that they will do it. Leaders, just like anyone else, want their group's approval and don't want to cause too much turmoil. Leaders too can settle. It takes courage to put your idea out there, and then let it be shaped and reshaped by the group, and it takes skill to draw people into the deeper conversations about the future. This especially takes courage when the psychic energy of the group is about closing down.

Second, it takes time to formulate a vision before it can be articulated. So many of our leaders have too many demands placed on them regarding immediate needs. Over time, all kinds of things have accrued to leadership that really don't have anything to do with it. Leadership teams need to name what is absolutely essential for them to do and what somebody else can do. I think it is important for leaders to say, "One of my key roles has to do with articulating a vision for religious life and creating a future when we can no longer take our future for granted. That is the work that is ours to do, if our group has decided that it wants a future." Some groups will go out of existence, and if the group has made that determination, then leaders need to put things into place to begin to close. But until a group has made that decision, the energy has to be about creating the future. I see too many leaders who are overwhelmed and tired and putting aside the kinds of things that would really energize them.

Third, I think that what creates passion and a willingness to sacrifice for the future is when people are in those places of great need. Unless you are in a place that requires a strong commitment to work for people in the margins and to do social critique, I don't know if this happens. You can't get that kind of passion by knowing about it vicariously. This doesn't mean that everyone needs to live in Haiti or the inner city, but we need to create some way to keep ourselves exposed to the great needs. Data from the Nygren-Ukeritis study indicates that a large percentage of members show little commitment to working with people who are poor or for systemic change. The data shows that religious have been absorbed into the dominant culture, often unaware of the degree of this absorption. Nygren and Ukeritis also say that few religious congregations have taken seriously the challenge of the finding, yet we call ourselves prophetic.

I think leaders need more social location among the great needs of the world in order to be able to articulate a vision for religious life. If we keep ourselves in settings where anyone else can do what we are doing, then why would we think there is a great need for the lifestyle? If anyone can teach at this school, or lead this hospital, or do whatever else we are doing, then we ourselves get confused about our role. The question for me that comes out of that is: Who are we without the works we have become famous for? We have to answer that question if we are going to have a future. I don't mean that we don't do work, but the question has to be: What is the work that nobody else is willing to do? For me, that is the essence of religious life. It is what our founders and foundresses did. They had the ability to see the work that needed to be done that no one else was doing, name it, and then bring others into that work.

What would you advise leaders who are trying to articulate a vision?

I would encourage them to create opportunities for members to have conversations with one another about who we are

without our works. Too many of us have been saying that
people don't need to come to religious life these days because
they can do the work they want to do outside of this life. This
gives us a big hint that we don't get the meaning of religious
life. We need to talk with one another about why we want to
be together in community and what being together in community means. How do we want to be together spiritually, and
what does being together spiritually mean? How do we discern
the great needs in light of our congregation's original story?
Until we talk about these questions together, I don't know
that we will have a future.

I get concerned when I work with religious congregations
and hear about the lack of energy. I don't think this is always
about age. I'm fully aware that people who are sixty-five don't
have the energy they had when they were forty-five, but I'm
not talking about that kind of energy. It's not a tiredness from
the work. It's the kind of tiredness that sets in when you don't
have a compelling vision. This is more of an apathy that we
translate into being tired. We hear people say things like, "I
just don't have energy for community," as if community were
an energy-taker, rather than an energy-giver. If we believed
that there was richness in community, then we would go after
it, no matter how tired we were.

We have to be courageous enough to say some of these
things to one another, because otherwise we are just going to
slide into a place to which we don't want to go. One of my
biggest worries about the future of religious life is that if we
don't do the work that we need to do to create a future, we will
just drift to a place that is our end. If we do absolutely everything we know how to do to create a future and then there is
no future, that's fine. But if we fail to do our part, then how
can God do God's part?

*Are you finding a hunger among religious today to have those
kinds of conversations and to do that kind of work?*

Yes, when I talk to religious, I sense a kind of reawakening of hope and fire. So, I think we want to do it. The function of good leaders is to help groups have the kind of conversation we want to have. It is a little awkward to talk about this, so it is not going to happen easily or without planning or structuring it. It may happen in little groups here and there, but it's a leadership function to get it to happen in the places where change can be propelled forward and with as many members as possible.

You mentioned that during these times, the psychic energy of groups is often about closing down. Have you found that this is common in religious congregations?

It's more common than I would like to acknowledge. On one hand, I say that because of people's faith, this is not about fear or security needs. On the other hand, I find that too often there is a passion missing. Where is our passion to assure the future of religious life—not for ourselves, but for the sake of God's people, the church, and the world? Do we have the passion that is part of the original fire of religious life for really making a difference in the world? I think if we had the passion of our radical founding, then we would be doing everything that we possibly could because that original fire is so needed by the world. I am concerned that even when we have the desire for a future, we may not have the will to do the things we need to do to make that future happen.

Would you give an example of this?

We do a lot of talking about community life. I hear people saying that they could try something new, or maybe discontinue living alone, and then five years later they are still saying the same things and are not making any moves. This is one of those times when we need to walk the talk. I think it's harder to do this now than it was in the past because we don't have the same internal pushes. During the 1950s and even into the '60s, each year a group of new members came out of the novitiate into the communities and ministry settings of the congregation. Groups had to re-form, re-negotiate, and think about how they wanted to be. We don't have that reality now. Some people can be in the same setting for twenty-five years, and there are no real external changes impinging on either the group or the individual. I think that now we have to say, even though we don't have that same structure, how can we get that same benefit in a freer way? We have to be more purposeful about many things. If we aren't, then we move into that "drift" that takes us to places where we don't want to go.

So, in this time of great change, what do you think members most want from leaders?

While I do think that members want personal attention and the care of their leaders—and that is valuable—I think that more importantly members want vision from their leaders. They want hope and challenge and they want support for a radical life. A sister recently said to me, "I am so tired of my leaders saying to me, 'Are you taking care of yourself?' What I want is to be supported and challenged to be in a radical place responding to unmet needs. I need encouragement to spend myself, not save myself." This is what I hear members asking for: to be challenged, and to be taken to a place that is a little bit more uncomfortable but full of purpose and meaning.

In the midst of these challenging times, do you ever wonder what it is that God desires for religious life?

I'm not sure what God wants for religious life, but I do know from our spiritual heritage that God wants people to live in solidarity with those who are most marginalized, who are most neglected, and who are most poor. As long as there are people with those needs then I think God desires for at least some people to respond in a way that is as radical as was Jesus' response to this reality. This is not to say that only religious need to respond in this way, but throughout the history of religious life when we have been most true to our core, this is what we have been doing. I don't know that God desires any particular form of religious life or tradition to survive, but history teaches us over and over that there have been people responding to the great needs with the kind of commitment of Jesus, and we keep calling the forms of commitment that have evolved "religious life." That's why I believe that even though some of the many forms of religious life that we now have may disappear, the essence of the life will burst into flame again.

I often quote this line of David Whyte to men and women religious, "Do you love your future?" Members of congregations need to dialogue on whether they love the future of religious life. Because if we loved it, I think we would do things differently. If we really loved it, we would have some passion about inviting people to join us. If we loved it, we wouldn't be letting it slip away so easily. If we loved it, we would be willing to try things we are not sure of.

What advice would you give leaders who are trying to find meaning in these times?

I would say to turn to the stories of exile in scripture, because they will find there a framework for what is happening today in religious life. In the exile we see the Hebrew people whose whole world fell apart, who lost all of the things that they had used previously to guide themselves and give themselves identity, and who struggled with what it meant to be God's people. Out of that experience was born a remnant of radical faithful people whom we love to talk about. I think that this is the spiritual vision that leaders can give to their members. This is a vision that can undergird the struggle and give us the spiritual nourishment needed to live in a time of exile. This hope is what prophets like Isaiah provided for the people in exile.

If we return to the question of what do members want of their leaders—they want spiritual leadership. They want to know how faith guides us through this kind of time. They want a spiritual framework for making the journey into the future. Leaders need to help create hope in the group that is not a "pie-in-the-sky" hope but the kind of hope that was born when the people sat by the streams of Babylon, hung up their harps, and wept because it was such a terrifying experience for them. After doing that, they could move forward. Sometimes I think that until we get to that place together, we won't really be able to create a future. We have to move to a place where the members don't see this time as just a personal, private disappointment that religious life didn't turn out differently, but rather as a group journey through exile that will give birth to something new.

When the exiles were down and out, had nothing, and were in a foreign land, Isaiah said, "Do you not perceive it? Are you not filled with hope of coming to be?" Leaders need to be making these kinds of connections for all of us, because we too are in a foreign land. This is a difficult time, and we need some kind of hopeful articulation of our future. That is the primary ministry of leaders.

9

Leadership and the Common Good

Lynn Jarrell, OSU

Many *religious congregations in the United States are facing one of the most dramatic periods in the history of religious life. The challenges of these times compel leaders to develop processes and decision-making tools that help their institutes focus on the common good. How do leaders enable their members to collectively define who they want to be and discern together the decisions before them?*

LCWR engaged canon lawyer **Lynn Jarrell, OSU,** *in a conversation on some of the serious concerns facing religious communities today and how leaders can help foster an emphasis on the common good as they deal with those challenges. In addition to serving in leadership of her own community, Lynn has been working with leaders of religious institutes throughout the United States and abroad for the last twenty-five years as a consultant, presenter, and teacher.*

You have been speaking to religious congregations across the country on the issue of the common good. How do you define this term?

I describe it as a three-part process of identifying the way we most want to be in light of our values, beliefs, and mission; taking into account our circumstances; and then responding appropriately to keep our focus on our desired ends. So it's a whole process of collectively weighing options and choosing our responses. It's not a one-time process, but rather a whole rhythm of life. New circumstances are always opening up and collective discernments may need to be revised and adapted. What ultimately doesn't change in the long run are the desired ends. If the process doesn't start with clarity on where we want to go and our desired ends, then our actions can easily become knee-jerk reactions that are very ungrounded.

The process also has to be done in a collective context. This doesn't mean that everyone in a group has to be directly in the conversation, but everyone must be at least aware of the process and willing to accept the outcome or response. Responding is the part that some groups don't like to do, or they respond to the easier situations or the immediate situations, instead of the ones that they really should be addressing.

What have you seen happening in religious life today that is causing the issue of common good to become a growing challenge?

First I would say that the dimension of the common good is a part of every group in society and all groups need to be aware of it. In this current time, I would say that a number of factors in religious life make attention to the common good challenging, especially: the declining number of members, the health of members, the aging of members, and the increasing number of options open to women to do good works.

Another big factor is our society's focus on individualization, which asserts the rights of all people to develop their unique capacities and skills. This has resulted in our becoming very sophisticated and having a strong sense of being independent persons. It can also result in people feeling that they don't need a group as much. This is a tension point. On one hand, our communities need developed persons. On the other hand, individualization colors how we enter into collective discernment. Power issues can surface here, where some people try to dominate a group. Yet, this is a fine line, since those who have a lot of talent will naturally lead a group. Can we accept being led by others?

Many congregations are inviting you to speak with them about the common good. What do you think is driving that?

I suspect that we are in a period where we feel we cannot control our environment like we used to do. That raises the question: What can we do to continue the life of a congregation? When I am with groups that have asked me to speak on this, our conversations usually lead to questions such as: What are our values? What choices can we make? What is our life together? Do we have a mission and, if so, what is it? Should we continue to remain actively engaged or should we disband? So I think it is a concern for survival that is driving interest in this topic, although I think the underlying questions have always been there. We just didn't talk about it so overtly.

I love conversation on this topic because it goes to the heart of our life. It really cuts away many of the other things that could cover up our need to look at why we live this life. What is happening in religious life is almost like what Jesus' death did for the disciples. It brought them into their true mission, which was to carry the Gospel message. But they had to go through the suffering to see that deeper purpose. There is a line in one of Mary Oliver's poems titled "At Black Rock" that reads: "I am reminded that resurrection only comes after the stone is rolled away from the tomb." It's as if you have to go through the death experience to understand the future. Death, however, is not a negative; death is a part of the cycle of life.

How does it feel for you to be at this moment in religious life when much is dying?

I feel tinges of sadness, because this is not what I thought it would be like when I joined religious life. There are increasingly fewer people with significant energy and creativity to help discuss these kinds of things and respond appropriately and sustain the life. But I wouldn't say that this is a frightening time. The question is more: How do I continue to engage with people who sustain my exploration of life and the discussion of that? That pool is becoming more and more limited. Sometimes the question arises: So why do I stay? That's not frightening, but just reminds me that something very significant is unfolding in this period of time and the question is: How can I delve into it?

How can religious life leaders help their members delve into what is unfolding today?

What's very clear is that there is no one answer. Probably five years ago I might have thought there was. I might have thought that if there were more education of the members or if we made significant changes, then we would have the answer. Now my thinking has evolved to understand that a leader herself needs to be learning about what is happening in our times and needs to be very much in touch with the world in an appropriate way. For example, leaders should be in touch with the development of globalization consciousness, the evolution of creation, political issues, immigration issues, and everything else that has significant impact on life today. Leaders also have to have a significant amount of energy, and I don't know if you can make that happen. Leaders need to practice good self-care but also recognize when they need to be resourced. Networking is the greatest resource I could suggest to them.

I also urge leaders to feel positive about God's hand in all of this. What we are experiencing today is not like depression; death is not depression. Rather, as I see it, it is a changing in the form and possibilities for how women and men can and need to live consecrated life in this postmodern period. This may make us feel sad and confused as previous practices and understandings are replaced.

Would you say that the questions that congregations need to ask themselves today about their identity and purpose—those things that help support a sense of the common good—are changing? What questions can help a congregation discuss the challenge of the common good?

I have to say honestly that this kind of conversation cannot necessarily be handled in all groups or by all leaders. Everything depends on the willingness and ability of the members, or at least a core group of members, to engage on that level. Often today the focus of leaders and/or the members in general is to put a huge amount of energy into maintenance—trying to help maintain individuals in fragile health either because of age or mental limitations. With such a focus and use of energy the institute may not be able to engage in this type of conversation in the intense manner that is needed. These kinds of conversations and questions call for a collective discernment if they are to have any real impact. A collective discernment around questions on identity and mission imply that a person is open and available for possible life changes or transformation. It could call people to a greater asceticism in their life, or acknowledging that the structures of authority in the congregation just don't work, or recognizing that a process of community living or some sort of clustering needs a whole different approach. A lot of our members may be at a point where they are comfortable and that sort of change would just be too difficult for them.

To work with the identity question requires a great availability to what is in the now and to the greater good of the group, and that may not be possible on a congregational level. It might be possible in different sections of the membership, but that requires that leaders be tuned into the possibilities of their members in light of their capacities and their stage of life. I find that some individual religious are very tuned into and interested in this kind of conversation, and those who are need to network and find others who want to talk like this. I find that conversations like these can be difficult within the boundaries of a congregation. Religious seem to have conversations like this across boundaries with members of other congregations, but at meetings of their own congregations, it is much harder to engage at that level. Perhaps it is due to a lack of trust or a lack of life connections.

What would you recommend to a leader who does want to engage her congregation in these conversations?

I would suggest that a leader take the members through the steps of the common good process. The group should name its desired ends and ask what is realistic for them as a group. The group needs to understand and accept its particular circumstances—financial, social, and so forth. Then the group needs to create a process that is appropriate to them that invites the members who are capable and truly open into a collective discernment that leads to making an appropriate response, knowing that the cycle of discerning is ongoing.

It's not that we have not been doing this all along. This is what chapters are about. But perhaps we have stylized chapters too much, or our members have become so sophisticated or overexposed to this that we have lost the impact of what a chapter could be about.

Our sense of identity is significantly changing, probably much faster than we could ever have imagined. This is partly due to the tremendous shifts occurring in our world. It is also due to the fact that there are now numerous ways in which God-centered services are being offered to people—ways that were not in existence even forty years ago. The other issue is our consciousness of and attention to the great value that contemplation can play in our lives. Although most of us were exposed to contemplation when we were in formation and have practiced it to some extent individually, we often do not have a collective sense of its power. Maybe we have not focused enough of our resources and time together to amplify this dimension of our lives as one of the primary expressions of who we are. So, the identity question is much less about doing as much as it is about being, and that is a major shift and a very hard conversation topic. It is fairly easy for us to speak about mission as being out there engaged in ministry, but to talk about our presence as our mission is much harder, other than doing it in just some pleasant words.

Why do you think that kind of conversation is so difficult?

I think because this is all so intimate to the person. It is also part of that individualization that has developed where the individual wants to protect his or her internal space and resists being dominated by another. We all know how hard this kind of faith conversation is, even with a spiritual director. The question is more about how we can share our faith life with one another. I do not have any strong clear answer on how to do that. I think each group needs to determine this for itself.

I also think that as our numbers become smaller, there is greater potential for having the kinds of connections with one another that are necessary for this collective cycle of seeking the group's common good. The largeness of our congregations was beneficial for making us a good work force, but has not been necessarily beneficial for the sustainability of the relationships among members, relationships that are needed in the common good process. Our commitment to one another in faith is about trust. We have to trust that we can be heard, but also that we support one another's journey in faith. This doesn't mean that we have to share all of our intimate life with everyone but that the trust exists.

I also think that even though we have greatly adapted the structures in religious life, many of them still prohibit our forming strong connections at the depth that I am describing. It's unintentional, but the structures are often very superficial, one of the primary ones being the concept of leadership authority. Even though we have all kinds of discernment processes in place, at least in theory, in the end there is usually one person or group with ultimate authority about how I spend my patrimony or how I make a decision about ministry. The style of religious life we are living is in a large sense still part of an established lifestyle recognized in the church and in society as acceptable from many centuries ago. This does not make it the only way or necessarily the way for our times. We know this but we continue often with practices and understandings that are not realistic or life sustaining. The invitation to us is to allow our expression of consecrated life to be a response to our times in light of who we have developed into and our circumstances.

Do you have a vision for another way of structuring religious life?

I think we have to let go of most of the structures that we have. This may very well mean that we have to wait for a whole generation to die off because we either have those structures so firmly in our head or we tell ourselves that we need them in order to take care of a large segment of our members. I do not agree with that perspective. I just think that we have not been able to think beyond how we can provide for those who cannot take care of themselves physically any longer and still begin to shape ourselves into a different way of being. That will require that most of us focus our attention on the group more than we might like to at this point in our lives, perhaps because of some ministry we are engaged in, or a living arrangement, or an energy path that we are in. We would have been willing to do this when we first joined, but we are not willing any longer, or we get animated at the thoughts of this at the time of a chapter, but then that desire dissipates quickly once the chapter closes.

Do you have any insight as to why that is?

Perhaps it is the structure that has caused us to disengage. For example, we elect a certain number of people to run the institute. If we are not part of that circle, either we may not feel any obligation to develop the new focus or we know that we are not part of the group that will make the decisions. Or, it could be that we have found our own world and our rhythm of life somewhere else that gives us a lot of meaning. It could also be that we see our mission as "out there," as opposed to focused on the internal life of the group. While that is very healthy, the truth is that there need to be internal connections to sustain a meaningful networking among the members. Any structures or ways of organizing the institute have the primary purpose of supporting such networking. Then it is up to the members to take advantage of the opportunities for building relationships with one another. Without such networking, any discussion of working for the common good will not give life to the members.

This is a true tension point that active institutes might experience more than monastic groups do. How can this happen with our geographic scattering, our busy work schedules, and a lack of regular connection, since often we just cross one another's paths at community meetings?

Can you give examples of some of the structures you think are problematic?

This would vary greatly from group to group, but, in general, I think many people feel disenfranchised from being able to effect any long-term change in their group. The problematic structures are not necessarily those required by canon law; they may be the common practices that have developed among a group. For example, members may raise chapter resolutions, or may serve on a committee that does a lot of work, but then they have to hand all that over to the leadership group that makes the final decision.

What do you think about the whole movement toward mergers and reconfigurations?

That's a very delicate conversation. From the perspective of the common-good process, reconfiguration or blending of groups can be a wonderful path for some. But at the heart of all of these decisions is the need to look at the question: How does this change enhance our desired ends? We also need to ask: How are we going to handle the internal reality of our diverse cultures? By this I mean the networking among members, things that will be altered in many ways—from the practical realities such as how do I get a car or to whom do I talk about a healthcare matter, to the bigger realities of operating chapters and assemblies or living with different people. So reconfigurations and mergers can be very life giving in theory—especially when such a change will give a group more people, save money, or provide a greater leadership pool—but the cultural and relationship dimensions can be hard in some cases.

It's important to remember that reconfigurations have been part of the whole history of consecrated life, so what we are experiencing now is just part of that whole rhythm. There have been studies that show that religious institutes usually go through a 300-year cycle, other studies say a 150-year cycle, and others say that 90 percent of the groups that exist now won't exist in fifty years. The studies vary, but I think all of them conclude that there is ultimately a rhythm to this.

It is not crucial to me that there be a structured collective expression of religious life. What's more important are two things. First, that those who are called to live a consecrated life live it in a way that's appropriate for their times.

Second, that those who live it, truly live it. My experience is that institutes and/or the members individually are not necessarily how they describe themselves in their documents. I am not saying this as a judgment, that this is good or bad, it is just what is. In fact, there may be some institutes or particular sections of institutes that are having a different experience of religious life than what I am talking about here. But what I see collectively is that what is written in our constitutions and chapter statements does not capture the spirit of how we are feeling called to live or actually choosing to live. This could be due to the structures in existence at the time our constitutions were approved or that our need for acceptance by church authorities prohibits us from perhaps saying or pursuing what we most believe. Or maybe we are no longer able to sit together collectively and express our deepest truths to one another and then find a concrete way of expressing these collective truths. This is painful, but it's part of the evolution and of entering into the realities of creation with its cycle. However, the end result, as I see it, is that if we are not attentive, we will not truly live the consecrated life in our times.

What signs of life and hope are you seeing these days?

I see some holy women who are truly on a spiritual journey. I see marvelous services going on. I see a great effort to pass on some of our lived experience and our resources to people who are taking up the work. Tremendous things are happening. But my experience is that many of us who are trying to live the life are not greatly nurtured by the life right now.

I was just with a wonderful community of women trying to look at their future, and they acknowledged all of the things that I just named. But, they kept saying, "There is a longing within us, and the longing has to do with our connection to one another." They finally phrased it in the question, "What do we hold in common?" One of their members said, "We have property in common, we have put our money together in common, we have a constitution in common, and we have a long tradition in common," and they all agreed to that. But they also agreed that there was a huge emptiness in them. I think that they were very honest in naming that desire for intimacy and in beginning conversations about their expectations of one another. This points to a whole other human dimension of our lives that we need to address—how do we respectfully challenge one another and stay connected with one another other than through our works?

So, while I see many, many great things happening, I also keep running into this longing and a drifting away. People are not necessarily leaving; they are staying but drifting from a connection with the group. And, in many cases, these are great people. So what is happening that we need to pay attention to? Is this calling us to live in a different way or perhaps to acknowledge that the practices we have just do not fit who we are? Again, none of that is negative. It's the challenge and the circumstances of our time and perhaps the invitation from God for our time.

So a leader is reading your words and says, "Yes, that describes my congregation. We are doing great works, but there is that longing among us." What could that leader do?

I would say: encourage. Encourage the development of the members' prayer lives, contemplation, and the discerning posture of the group. This is where God's grace will speak to us. We cannot make this happen, just like we can't make vocations happen. We cannot make anything happen, although we used to think we could. Now we seem more aware that we need to be in a waiting posture. Perhaps it would be helpful to reflect on Mary. She accepted something that was totally confusing to her, waited, and shared that waiting with Elizabeth. I would encourage leaders to call on Mary or others who have gone before us such as Martin Luther King Jr. or Gandhi. We can draw upon these people to help us with our waiting and hoping, but not grasping. This is a great time for the spiritual life.

Why is that?

Because we are being stripped down in so many ways. It's almost as if we are being invited to be in increasing harmony with what Earth is suffering at this time with the climate warming, the refugee camps of displaced persons, the struggle of immigrants. It's almost like a gift from God to be stripped like this, but that doesn't necessarily make it less painful.

So, I say to leaders: try to keep focusing on what's most important, resource yourself, and engage fully with people who can enhance your vision and accept the reality that if the cycle of life is calling your institute into fully letting go, then move into that process actively instead of denying or avoiding the transformation at hand.

10

Leaders as Agents of Transformation

Judy Cannato

 *As the global community explores new paradigms for understanding our fundamental connectedness, the creation of new ways of relating to one another becomes imperative. How can leaders help inspire their members for this critical effort and engage members in the work of transformation of themselves and the world?*

Author **Judy Cannato** *explored some of these concepts in her books, which include* Radical Amazement: Contemplative Lessons from Black Holes, Supernovas, and Other Wonders of the Universe, *and* Field of Compassion: How the New Cosmology Is Transforming Spiritual Life. *Because of the resonance so many LCWR members felt with her work, we asked her to reflect on the spirituality and practices that could help us contribute to the transformation of the world. Although she had been battling cancer, Judy accepted an interview with LCWR. Within weeks after the interview, Judy's condition significantly worsened, and she died shortly afterward.*

Those of us in religious life today ask ourselves about the significance of this life in today's reality. We recognize that women religious are one among many groups and organizations trying to meet the massive needs of the world today, and we wonder what is the unique contribution that we, as a body of intentionally spiritual women, can make to meeting the unmet needs of the contem-

porary world. What insights can you offer us that might help us to explore this question?

First, I must acknowledge my own immersion in the Universe Story, and that is the perspective from which I am responding to your questions. The Universe Story is dynamic, evolutionary, resonant with our Christian tradition—and it offers fresh images and insights that can inspire us in a time when, as you say, the needs of the world are massive. Certainly the needs are massive, but I think almost all the crises are fallout from a worldview that no longer serves us, a mechanistic view that pictures creation as an assembly of disconnected pieces and parts. Our culture still functions out of this paradigm, even though we have known for over a century that this is not so. The Universe Story so clearly demonstrates what the mystics of our tradition have said all along, that all life is connected on a fundamental level, that all is one.

Consumerism, greed, fundamentalism—all those social forms and behaviors that do such violence to our planet and to our companions here on Earth—in one way or another assert that we are disparate pieces and parts rather than fundamentally connected. I think a unique contribution a body of intentionally spiritual women can make is to help usher in this new paradigm, which will fundamentally alter not only the way we think but will radically change the way we relate to one another. This is the world's most desperate need—and that is where women religious have always responded. Where the need is great, their love has always been greater.

You speak of how the stances of spaciousness, contemplation, commitment, and imagination can contribute to the transformation of the world. You also speak of how our capacity to influence change in the world is stronger when it is exercised with others who have the same intentions. These four stances are inherent in religious life—and are lived out communally. From your experience with women religious, what would you say to us about the potential we have, through the structure of our religious lives, to contribute to the transformation of the world?

The vows of women religious are essentially an expression of the desire to live in non-attachment, to remain free from entanglements, however worthy, that require time and energy. Spaciousness, contemplation, commitment to the whole, and imaginative vision can flow more easily from those who live in non-attachment. I am not saying that only religious can live this way, for many of us, regardless of our lifestyle, desire this kind of life. But it seems to me that women religious have an edge that enables you to be quite spacious, making room not only for others but for the new, for whatever is emerging at this moment in history.

The contemplative stance, essentially the capacity to be aware of love's presence everywhere, is one that is fundamental to discerning what is emerging from the spaciousness and the knowing how to respond. The willingness to risk our energies requires commitment—not commitment to a particular lifestyle, but commitment to the voice of the Spirit, which at times may appear to stand in contradiction to anything we've imagined before. This all requires engagement of the imagination and trust that the imagination is fueled by the Spirit. Transformation must now occur on a global level. Who better to respond to this challenge than women religious who are a world-wide force, a powerful force, that has always been engaged in transformation?

You speak of increased numbers of people moving into higher stages of development that allow them to see the whole of life more clearly, who live out of a sense of the interconnectedness of all things, whose loving embrace of life is wide enough to hold all of reality. It would seem that a religious life of the future could be a natural place where persons who intentionally wish to move into these stages of development might be drawn. Do you have any insights to share around that possibility that could help us envision religious life in new ways?

Another way to speak of these higher stages of development is in terms of a sense of ever-greater connectedness. This is happening as we move into the new paradigm. Or perhaps it is better to say that the new paradigm is the result of the collective experience of connectedness. Just as the motive for many who have entered religious life in the past was to live out of ever-deepening faith, which is to say, to live out of a higher consciousness, I think it is possible for those entering religious life in the future to be moved by the call to intentional growth in consciousness.

But we must also remember that our growth and development usually happen while we're busy about something else. In simply living life, employing our gifts that the Gospel might be enfleshed, and experiencing the clashes with others and with ourselves that occur—in all that activity we have the raw material for transformation. We reflect upon what we experience, and if we have as our intention and framework what occurs in the context of evolution of consciousness, then it is more likely to occur. The possibility of religious communities being intentional about conscious evolution excites me—but we must always remember that such evolution is also the work of the Spirit. I already see this kind of movement among women religious all over the world, and I think the fact that so many are trying to get a handle on it is a sign the Spirit has already invited us into this work.

You describe the impetus within the human being to become something more. Women religious are consciously trying to plan for a future where we can be something more for the world and, as we do so, stay open to possibilities beyond our present knowing and which are, accordingly, elusive to planning. For leaders in religious life, this poses a particular challenge as they live in the intersection of needing to vision and plan for the future of their institutes and yet also live in a place that Rahner describes as "the loving acceptance of mystery and its unpredictable disposal of us." What can you say to religious congregation leaders who live in that daily tension of planning and desiring to be held in mystery's unpredictable disposal?

Maintenance of institutes and planning for the future are nonnegotiables and certainly made challenging as the number of sisters in active ministry decreases and the number of aged sisters increases. It seems as if that will be a major part of the experience of religious life for at least a few more decades. One of the blessings of community life is the diversity of gifts. Among the members there are the practical ones and there are the dreamers, and all the nuances in between, and that enables the united response as many come together for the sake of the common good. I hope that doesn't change, that there is the recognition and celebration of diversity within community.

I like the Buddhist reflection that says, "Before enlightenment, chop wood, carry water. After enlightenment, chop wood, carry water." While the tasks remain the same, everything is changed, depending on the paradigm out of which you operate. While for some it may be possible to have work that actively or overtly engages the new paradigm, for others the call is to deal with the practical with a new set of lenses. Knowing that all manifestation comes from the way we think, the most critical piece is to be aware of our awareness, the level of consciousness we bring to all we are about.

What I am trying to say is that the way you frame any task is as significant as the task itself. To look at responsibilities through the lens of "everything is connected" and "all is one" can bring a new depth of love and compassion to them. We still chop wood and carry water but from a transformed perspective.

You note that the transformation of the world is not going to take place through the efforts of exceptional superheroes, but rather though the efforts of ordinary human beings. You also affirm that we are already equipped for the task—we have stories to move us and images to engage us for the work ahead. How do you think leaders today can best help their membership believe in their ca-

pacities for the daunting challenges that are ahead, and how can they best use stories and images to engage their members in the work of transformation?

Perhaps one of the most significant roles of leadership is to be the storytellers and the story keepers. It is necessary to hear the "old" narratives unpacked in ways that are truly life giving, and it is also necessary to engage new stories that contribute to our own evolution. In *Field of Compassion*, for example, I try to demonstrate how the Universe Story can illuminate our understanding of the narratives central to our Christian tradition. The Universe Story in and of itself moves us toward transformation, but it also allows us to see our tradition in a new light, and that too is transformative.

If the stories we tell are vital, if they vibrate with creative energy, they move us to see the greater vision, but they also move us to see the truth about ourselves—that we are co-creators empowered by the Spirit to be instruments of transformation.

Your understanding of resurrection as an image for new awareness, as an awakening to the unknown, seems to resonate with the transformation occurring within religious life today. The radical changes we are experiencing may be leading us to such an awakening. But you also remind us that death is the prerequisite for the experience of resurrection. Deaths of all types are prevalent within the reality of religious life, sometimes making the promise of resurrection difficult to trust. What can you say to us about sustaining ourselves through the dying processes of these times?

There comes a moment in the death-resurrection experience in which there is a shift from doing what we know will sustain us to allowing ourselves to be sustained by Holy Mystery. At the beginning of the process we begin to notice a change. Before long, we begin to plot the trajectory, see the possible or probable manifestations, and act in responsible ways toward that which has been entrusted to us. But then a subtle shift occurs. Having spent our energies in the effort to sustain the old, we recognize the encroachment of death nevertheless.

We step away from doing what sustains us to simply surrender to that which sustains—the Spirit at work among us. This is the necessary preparation for resurrection—the complete and total surrender of all that has been, even all that has been imagined and hoped for. It is tempting to read the Gospel accounts and think that resurrection is instantaneous, but in my experience it normally is not. There is a period of "I don't know," perhaps creating the necessary space for completely letting go. "I don't know" if we will live or die. "I don't know" if religious life will continue or not. "I don't know" what Holy Mystery is doing. All that remains is the experience of the present moment—and trust. This may sound negative or frightening. But in truth it is an exquisite knowing nothing but the love of the Holy One. Making no effort to sustain what has been, we free the Spirit to work in and through us. To be open to resurrection takes courage, because we must face our darkest fears and allow ourselves to deeply trust in the Holy One. It is the Spirit's work, and the process is a reminder that, although we are certainly co-creative participants, more than anything we ourselves are the Spirit's work.

You have written so openly and honestly about your own experience with illness and the wisdom you have drawn from that experience. Is there anything more that you can share with us about what you have learned since you wrote about it in Field of Compassion*?*

One of the lessons that has been reaffirmed is that what is most significant is how we frame our experiences. During these past two years I have tried to see all that is happening as an invitation to growth in consciousness. That helps this become a communal as well as personal experience. I try to ask myself questions: What is the possibility of conscious evolution here in this moment? Where do I see Holy Mystery sustaining me, and how do I want to respond? I try to observe, to be attentive, as awake and aware as I can be—without judging anything, least of all myself. I try not to judge my fear or the past or my shortcomings. To the best of my ability I simply accept who I am—a manifestation of incomprehensible Holy Mystery, limited and limitless, powerful and powerless. I try to surrender in trust and allow myself to receive love in all the ways it comes. I have learned that every moment of life is grace, a beautiful gift of love—and a Holy Mystery.

From your interaction with women religious, is there a challenge that you think would be helpful to offer us? Is there anything that you have observed that you would draw our attention to with the hope that it would help us to contribute more effectively to the transformation of the world?

Yes. I would like to issue the challenge in the form of a story I heard from Isha Judd:

> A king was given a gift of two falcons. Soon he became accustomed to seeing one of the falcons in flight each day, its wings outstretched as it soared on the wind. One day he asked his falconer, "Were there not two falcons given as gift?"
>
> "Yes," the falconer replied, "but the second falcon refuses to fly. It is healthy, its wings intact. It is well fed. Still, with all the coaxing, the second falcon refuses to fly. It simply sits on its perch all day."
>
> The king instructed the falconer to speak to the farmer, a simple yet wise man, to see if he could help resolve the dilemma.
>
> The next morning the king was delighted to see two falcons, wings outstretched, soaring upon the

wind. The king asked the farmer, "How were you able to do what the best of falconers, with all his coaxing, could not do?"

"Simple," replied the farmer," I sawed off the branch."

Perhaps one way of looking at what is occurring in religious life is to say that the branch has been sawed off. The comfortable and familiar are gone, but there is new opportunity for flight—for the engagement of creativity and gifts and evolutionary impulse in ways never before imagined.

My challenge: On behalf of humankind, fly!

11

Leaders' Roles in Encouraging Members to Dream and Vision Their Future

Lynn Levo, CSJ

 *Women religious find themselves in a place where much of what they have known about religious life is now ending, and what the life will be in the future is not yet clear. In this interview, **Lynn Levo, CSJ**, a licensed psychologist, consultant, and lecturer, with experience as a leader in her own community, speaks of the importance of engaging members in actively imagining a different future, particularly at this unique time. How might a leader foster this type of dreaming and visioning among members, and how might leaders nurture and harness the energy of their own dreams?*

If one of the first steps in creating a future is to imagine it, how important is it that women religious be encouraged to dream of what they wish for and believe in for the future—their own future and that of their congregations?

The first thing that comes to mind for me is Proverbs 29:18: "Without a vision, the people perish." It is important to think about where we want to go and where we are being called and what is God trying to gift us with at this time. I think it is important to distinguish between dreaming and visioning. To dream is to imagine something as possible and give free reign to one's imagination. To vision is to take the dream and make it a reality. Visioning is about trying to imagine what is possible and making it happen. Dreams and visions are a clue to who we really are and who we can become.

How important is it to actively imagine ourselves into our future, particularly at this time in religious life when so little is mapped out for its future?

We have to look at the time we are in. It is a very rapidly changing time and really an ending time. When I say that, it doesn't cause me to feel hopeless or anxious. It's just that a lot of what we have known is ending, and the new is not yet coming. So it can be a very exciting time for us because we have to figure out who we are and where we are being called.

There are, however, some natural tendencies that are not helpful that occur at disturbing times. One tendency is not to attend to what is happening, where we tune out and go our merry way. Another is to be taken over and paralyzed, especially with fear and anxiety. And a third is to try to just keep things the same.

I think it is important to realize too that we are already operating out of a vision—a vision that may not be the best vision for us and is likely unconscious. I think the vision we have now is based on a lot of dualisms that we have learned along the way, particularly since we are heavily ensconced in our culture and in the church. This dualistic vision tends to split things into what is good and what is not. During anxious and distressing times, we can become rigid in our thinking and believe that there are right and wrong ways of doing things, including how to live religious life. So, perhaps it is not that we are living without a vision, but rather we are being challenged today to look at the vision we are living out of and realize that it is not the holistic vision of the Gospel. It is a vision that doesn't really help us be who we want to be, who we are called to be.

I also think that we tend to plan our dreams and visions rather than to listen for them, which is a different process. One of the challenges in religious life now is to deal with our being so busy and so into doing. I'm not sure that we take the time to really listen for where we are being called. David Tracy says that the West has taught us how to breathe out, which is about responding to, giving, and serving. While we don't want to belittle these things, in times of great upheaval it is especially important to also breathe in. This requires our developing our interior life and spirit, not just individually, but collectively. Do we need to be better listeners to dreams and visions?

What does a vision help us to do? With what can it provide us?

A vision helps us look at our purpose, and in particular, it can help us to focus our energy as a community to fulfill our purpose. One of the wise women in my congregation said that "religious life exists to say that something is possible in each era in which it is lived." So we need to ask: What are we supposed to say is possible for this era? And, we need to see how this becomes part of our purpose for leading this not-ordinary life. A vision makes us pay attention to our purpose and make it become a reality. The vision becomes a North Star that can guide our decisions at every level and help us prioritize and clarify our values. Values are always connected to money and doing, so they impact where we place our limited resources.

Vision, especially in situations where people are engaged in helping create the vision, can raise the sights of everybody in the community and get us to look at things differently. It can help us displace complacency, especially if the vision touches on the charism or foundational story. Vision can provide motivation and help the routines of our lives become more meaningful. Vision can also increase our awareness of a range of possible futures and expand our capacity to move into the future. Visioning can also be a way to find common ground among a group that often has diverse interests and can help hold us together, especially in difficult times.

How does the current state of religious life in the United States affect the way women religious dream and plan for our future?

I think it can have both a plus and a minus effect. On the one hand, rather than do the important work of grieving the losses during this time of ending and loss, people can tune out and get angry. Some of us are getting mad instead of sad. It would be helpful if we could be sad and grieve the losses while maintaining hope in the promise that we will not be abandoned. There also can be a seeking of comfort or complacency that lets us just enjoy where we are and not have to worry about or plan for the future.

On the other hand, I sense among women religious a great yearning for more, even though our members are getting older. We are older, and I think wiser and, as a result, less cautious, at least at times, and more willing to take some risks. There is a real desire to be authentic. We also seem to be less at odds with one another within congregations, and there is less competition among congregations. We are realizing that we are all in this together.

This is an ending time, a dramatically changing time not just for us but in the world in general, and sometimes we don't seem to realize that. I think it is a time when God is trying to gift us with our humanity and that is not easy for us or for others. We are called to be more vulnerable and to deal with loss and sadness. This is why we need to pay more attention to the interior life, both personally and communally. Taking a good look at and understanding what is happening around us, remaining hopeful, and paying attention to the deeper parts of ourselves become critical.

What do you find gets in the way of our dreaming and visioning?

One thing would be uncertainty. A lot of us want to be sure that we are on the right path, that we have made the right decision. Another is time and money. Sometimes a vision requires an expenditure of money, and it can require time together if we are to slow down and do this process together. I think lack of information about these dramatic times and about the possibilities gets in the way. This is an area where leadership can take a role in providing members with the needed information, calling members to see the bigger picture. I also think negative attitudes get in the way. We need to deal with those harder feelings (e.g., loss, anxiety, fear, discouragement), or they can take over.

How important is it for a congregation to have dreams if it wishes to bring in new members? What can a congregation's corporate dreams say about its coherence and vitality as a group?

What I would say about new members goes for current members, too. I think it is about hope. Real hope looks at the world as it is, accepts it, but is not resigned to it. Hope leads to what we call psychological and emotional resiliency, which helps us to be more mentally, physically, and emotionally prepared to deal with what comes. As people try to implement a vision, there will be challenges and maybe some regrets. Hope gives us resiliency and a capacity to bounce back and not be taken down by something that is a challenge or something that is not going right. Hope also leads to positive emotions and thoughts, increased coping abilities, and decreased depression. Those are critical factors when trying to not only create a vision, but to implement it and live out of it. We need a positive, hopeful attitude and a sense that things will go right. All of this impacts our openness; our flexibility of thinking; our capacities to problem solve, empathize and persist, and our willingness to seek variety.

All of this can help us as we welcome new members. It is important that new members see that we have a vision and that we can flexibly respond when they see things in another way or raise a different perspective. We all need to be able to walk in one another's shoes.

What could a congregation's members learn from one another in sharing their dreams?

First, I think it is a false notion that we do not need one another. In our culture that promotes individualism, as well as an exaggerated notion of privacy, we can easily fall into this same kind of thinking. We become our best self in relationship with others. We can also have a better picture of reality when we are in dialogue with one another. When we share with one another about our possible future, the dreaming will become more realistic and possible because we are doing it from a variety of perspectives. There is a lot more to life than one's own perspective, and if a system becomes too homogenous, it is very vulnerable to environmental shifts or changes, because the system does not have as much flexibility or diversity.

Our congregations have more diversity now, and we have already been dealing with the shifts and changes. This has given us a greater capacity to move forward. When there is diversity, innovative solutions for getting to the vision can at least be put on the table. Margaret Wheatley has said, "No one person is smart enough to design anything for the whole system." I think that is true and that the only way we can create a vision for the whole is to engage everyone as much as possible.

How can women religious leaders encourage their members to be active, self-confident, and purposeful about imagining a future for themselves, for their congregations, and for religious life as a whole?

I like this question because it relates to the members' own future. Each one of us has to be imagining our own future and listening to hear the authentic invitations for us. How we do that together as congregations and with other congregations impacts religious life. Margaret Wheatley also says that every person is a visionary and that every person wants to create a world where she can thrive. I think that is true, although not everyone acts out of that. People learn that it is not true, but that is a false learning. Circumstances lead people to believe that they don't have anything to say about their lives and that is sad. Each of us also needs to believe that something more can be accomplished by joining with others.

This is where women leaders can encourage their members by helping to create conditions that help people to dream both individually and collectively. One of the elements that is essential to corporate visioning is trust. Individuals also need to learn to trust the process. Whenever we try to engage one another about our future, we need to believe that wisdom and guidance will come to us if we collectively place ourselves in a listening mode to the Spirit in and among us. We are more likely to plan ourselves into a vision than to listen for it and respond to it, and I do not believe that this is the best thing to do at this point. We are often too rational, and I don't think that this is what will move us forward.

Again, Margaret Wheatley has said that "understanding an emerging world asks us to stand in a different place, to be willing to be involved in discovery and to participate more than plan." The question for leaders is how do they help women in their congregations to realize that we are in an emerging world, that it is not here yet, and that we are planting the seeds. We are great planners, but I am not sure that we are good at listening. We have to recognize that this is a strange, uneasy time, and we need to believe that God is trying to gift us at this time, through some challenging and difficult circumstances. Suffering and diminishment are not easy things, but somehow that is where the gift is coming from.

How can leaders help members create, realize, and perhaps re-configure their goals and dreams?

We have to pay attention to the world in which we live and understand the driving forces that are impacting us and everything around us. So we have to be grounded in what is happening in the world. Two of my favorite questions to ask are: Who have we learned to be? We have learned a lot and some of it is unconscious. We need to know our stories. And, who are we called to be now? This is the transformative question.

I think that we are at a juncture. We need to look at our core values and fundamental beliefs. And then we have to encourage one another to be still, to give the Spirit a chance to surface and influence us.

How can we help one another deal with the fear that can arise in this time?

Fear can totally derail us because its basic message is: I'm not safe or we're not safe. So, how do we recognize fear and how do we address it and not let it take over? Jesus said again and again, "Do not be afraid." He knew that fear could be a major motivator that could shut us down. Leaders need to help members recognize and talk about their fears. And it is also important for leaders to remember that if you let a group do its thing, it will make riskier decisions than its members would as individuals. Leaders have to be prepared for a visioning group going for it in bigger ways than they may have imagined. How does a leader not become afraid when the group vision turns out to be grander than that of the leaders and includes more of the world in its embrace than the leaders might have anticipated? This requires that leaders take a long, loving look at the real, be honest, and be able to state what is. At the same time, they have to believe that despite some difficult and challenging circumstances, their congregations can live the vision.

Lastly, I think that leaders have to be about connections, fostering connections between and among their members. Leaders can enhance visioning by increasing the number, strength, and variety of connections. Leaders have to be about fostering relationships—among the members, between themselves and their members, and with other groups as well. Co-laboring is not optional.

How can leaders harness the resources of their own dreams?

The number-one thing is that leaders include themselves in all that we talked about. A leader's personal dreams and visions are absolutely essential. We are so programmed to believe that if we deal with ourselves personally we are being selfish. We don't understand the notion of self-reference. A self-referenced person knows what she thinks, feels, wants, needs, and dreams, and is able to respond to what others think, feel, want, and need. We almost attach sanctity to paying attention to the other, and as soon as we start focusing on ourselves we hear the word "selfish"—and that is killing us. Leaders need to believe that they do not give up their hopes and dreams while they are in leadership because those hopes and dreams are where their passion comes from. And you want people with passion in leadership. Leaders need to make connections with others, take time off, and do those other good self-care things that promote their own personhood. And this can be contagious.

I think we have to remember that participation in processes of visioning is not a choice. If leaders want members to buy into the vision and try to make it a reality, then they have to involve them as much as possible. I think a leader's role is to invite people to rethink and redesign what is needed to achieve the vision. If more people are involved, then more people will help to create a future that has them in it and will try to make it happen. If they are not in the visioning, then they are not going to make it happen. What can occur then is that people don't just remain neutral, they may even become oppositional. If leaders get people involved, then they will not be spending their energy trying to sell the members on an idea or figuring out how to give them an incentive so that they will agree. Leaders do better putting their energy into involving people in making the vision happen versus trying to convince people that this is the right thing to do. People usually support what they create. So, keep asking: How can we involve as many people as possible? We know that some people do not want to be involved and have given up the ship. Leaders have to go with those who can move forward.

Leaders also have to expect a reaction to a vision. Some of it will be positive, and some of it won't be. Don't be caught off guard and surprised that not everybody will be on board. There is a big difference between handing people a plan and inviting people to create a vision together. Engaging people in the process will lessen the reactions.

It is important to remember the value of dialogue. We all see the reality we want to see, and we all create our own interpretations. We have to make sure that we have conversations so that we hear one another and begin to understand the other's perceptions. Giving and getting as much information as possible is also important. In the past, only those who needed to know got the information. But if we are going to be creative and able to respond in this changing, challenging time, then we should give people as much information as possible. Don't withhold. The more information people have and the more enriching the information is, then the more people are going to be able to make good decisions. Actions that evolve from vision flow on their own energy. When people are forced to do something or it is imposed on them, the action quickly loses power. Fear and guilt lose their power as motivators as well.

Once a group establishes a vision, what can they do next?

This is where we use the skills that we already have. We can set reasonable and measurable goals and objectives, create a map for making the vision a reality, and track success. What leaders can do is to keep articulating the vision frequently and defend it when necessary. It is good to remind people what they are moving toward and what the result or reward will be. It is helpful as well for leaders to recognize what people are going through, since the journey toward a vision can, at times, be painful, especially since it often involves letting go and loss.

What could LCWR do to foster this kind of visioning for the future?

I think it would be helpful if leaders could talk more about the time in which we are living and speak of it frankly as a time of ending and change. We have to be able to say that we have no idea what religious life will look like in the future. We know that congregations are getting smaller, that they are aging, that we have fewer women religious than we would like. Could LCWR help us understand this in a context? We are living in a time where we are seeing that the major institutions of the world don't work. Enron doesn't work, the government doesn't work, the church doesn't work, and this is our reality. It is helpful to remember that we need not feel guilt or shame over the shortage of women religious or the diminishment. Not that we did not have any part in it, but it has been coming for a long time.

I think, too, that we are being handed our humanity. How can LCWR help us see this? As adult human beings, we have adult human needs that are not optional and that must be met in our communal life of service. How do we have those needs met and still be women of service and women of the Gospel? I think at this time, we may be too externally focused, too busy doing. We need to breathe in as well as to continue the breathing out that we are so good at doing. It's a question of balance.

LEADING THROUGH CHANGE

12

Unearthing the Potential of Uncertain Times

Donna M. Fyffe

Donna M. Fyffe *is president of Community-Works, Inc., an international consulting practice located in Indianapolis, Indiana. Her expertise resides in community building, leadership development, and cultural change. She works extensively with congregations of women religious and with faith-based and educational institutions.*

Because of the tremendous amount of change and loss being experienced by U.S. women religious today, LCWR asked Donna to reflect on how to lead through a period of deep uncertainty. What kind of inner disciplines can help leaders and those they lead sustain themselves in times of chaos and change? What personal qualities might leaders intentionally try to develop to help them effectively lead in uncertain times? What are the key questions leaders should ask themselves when encountering a period of profound uncertainty?

Political scientist Thomas Homer-Dixon says that "we need to know in our bones that we ride the razor's edge between order and chaos," and that to "truly know we inhabit such a world makes us more resilient." Would you see such a mindset helping women religious leaders at this time when much of what we have known in life is breaking down?

Homer-Dixon has some underlying assumptions behind this statement that would be helpful for us to understand. In his writings, he speaks to the complexity of our world realities, a complexity that impacts our daily world. He notes that while connectivity is viewed as a virtue in a complex reality in times of crisis (tightly coupled, circle the wagons), the system collapses—catastrophe. To be resilient in this time of crisis, Homer-Dixon notes that we need a better balance of self-sufficiency and interdependence and we need collaboration among diverse interests. Both of these capacities are constantly being refined among women religious.

A place of hope in his thinking is that there is a normalcy in the breakdown of systems. What we know is that following breakdown there is rebirth and renewal. This occurs through a system's capacity for being adaptive, creative, and able to do reformative work. Given the more than fifty years of renewal that religious life has experienced, here is the razor edge of choice. Will women religious see, believe, and go into the place of rebirth—into the chaos?

Dixon notes that as humans we don't choose to embrace system breakdown or change. His observation is that "we cherish our systems and we want them to be permanent; we haven't really understood that our challenge isn't to preserve the status quo but rather to adapt to, thrive in, and shape for the better a world of constant change."

What does this take? A mind not fixed on the status quo, but rather a mind and attitude that is "comfortable with constant change, radical surprise, even breakdown...and must constantly anticipate a wide variety of futures." Clearly this is the place of possibility thinking.

Dixon's quote is really about the capacity to see the complexity of our world, to embrace the reality of change. It's about holding in balance self-sufficiency and interdependence, the individual and the community. For women of Spirit, open to the God of surprise, the God who creates out of chaos, the God of constant change allowing us to continually evolve, this is no surprise.

Talk about being prophetic! Dixon is putting before women religious what you know deep in your bones. You see the world unfolding right before your eyes. There is a freedom within religious life to be open to constant change, to delight in radical surprise, to have the capacity and courage to cross thresholds bridging breakdown and renewal and co-create with God what is yearning to be birthed today.

Now, does everyone get this and want this? No. I truly believe that "No" is real. Yet, at the same time, I also believe that members want their leaders to call them to this because in the deepest recesses of their hearts they want mission, their charism, and the Gospel to flourish and shape the world.

So much is changing and being lost all around us—parts of the ecosystem, cultures, and more. Some people respond to this kind of massive loss by holding on to a fixed view of things, to something that is known and certain. Do you see that tendency in religious life and, if so, what are its effects?

Our world has changed and is changing. Over the last more than fifty years women religious have lived constantly with change. Like the world about them, they have dealt with the change in society, our church, the world, and the universe. Some women religious readily embrace change, others lead the change, and, of course, some hold the line on change. We see the internal loss of a clearly defined way of living religious life. Clarity is waning about one's relationship with the church, theology, ecclesiology, cosmology—everything is changing. How change is handled or coped with is dependent on its level of impact, one's perspective on change, and the maturity of the group in dealing with change. Groups can feed one another's desire for change and movement. Groups can also feed fear and anxiety, retarding change.

Women religious, like their lay counterparts, can hold on to a fixed view of things. They can hold on to "perceived certainty" and deny their reality. What is lost is the gift, capacity, and insight to see the innovation and creativity in the change. They fail to see the possibilities and how to bring their life into the times we are living in. For example, at this moment in history, the majority of women religious are older adults. Pretending to be young is to miss owning the gifts of wisdom, integration, and influence that come with age and maturity.

What if the work of women religious is to create deeper insight; reframe what is; see reality differently; generate greater consciousness; go to people's blind spots and uncover values, beliefs, the Christ within? What if their work is one of integrity, being in the place of mystery and grace, so that they can influence social transformation and co-create with God what is needed for these times?

Resistance occurs during times of change. Think of times when you've moved to a new location; changed your ministry; experienced rituals/prayer different from how you like to pray; and engaged in conversations that questioned your values, beliefs, and perhaps your core identity. All of this could actually be very good. In fact, for some, these changes might be life giving while at the same time generating feelings of loss and resistance. What is key is to allow ourselves to feel all our feelings—those of pain and those of joy—and to acknowledge and grieve the loss we are feeling. The degree to which we will change or be adaptive, that is, find new ways to live within our changing environment, is contingent on our ability to recognize our fear and our anxieties and to deal with them.

What are the effects of holding on to a fixed view of things? A congregation becomes antiquated, non-relevant, and loses its capacity to be about mission in today's world.

Many people seem to think that the way religious life has been lived in the past probably will not be the way it will be in the fu-

ture, yet they don't know what the new ways might be. What do you recommend for how to live without anxiety and with hope in that in-between time?

First and foremost, I would banish this statement. Women religious need to name the life that is. They need to name what is essential to them and what that looks like as they live faithfully day in and day out. To live in what Lynn M. Levo, CSJ, calls a place of "nowhere between two somewheres" is not healthy. It stifles resiliency, vitality, and hope because it holds people in suspension. People are being asked to keep looking back to what was. And people are constantly reminded of the unknown, fostering doubt and uncertainty. All of us need to name the life that is and to make choices each day about the life we want now and for those who follow. Each day, we are creating the future we want by the decisions we make and the actions we take.

I'm not sure we can be freed of anxiety. What we can do is notice what triggers our anxiety; notice it and how it is making us feel. If we can put the situation outside of ourselves and look at it objectively, we can see the assumptions and the mental models that are holding us captive. It takes spiritual discipline to be non-anxious. If we strive to follow this discipline of noticing and living in the now, we will be comfortable with who we are, at one with our inner truth, and be a non-anxious presence. All of this calls for a profound trust that God is ever present within us.

What normally sustains people in times of chaos?

I asked a friend who is a woman religious what sustains her in times of chaos. She said she had just recently watched again the video of the four women religious leaders from New Orleans who spoke at the 2006 LCWR assembly and noted what sustained them. It was knowing who they were (their identity as women religious) and their purpose (or mission), who God was in their lives (personal and communal), contemplation (putting all in God's hands), and a supportive community and supportive relationships.

I affirm what she says. The one thing that consistently sustains me above everything else during my own times of anxiety and fear is my belief in and relationship with God. The other thing that I'm learning about when dealing with chaos, confusion, and grief is the importance of having the inner freedom to allow myself to be disturbed. For it is in this place of being disturbed that I can break patterns that keep me stuck. I can see into my blind spots and make new choices. I can actually find stability in the disequilibrium. This is not easy. For me, it takes incredible spiritual discipline.

Perhaps this can be articulated in a different way. What sustains people in times of chaos is dependent on how much inner discipline they have. Are they able to identify, tolerate, and manage what they are feeling? If yes, then the chaos doesn't leak out and infiltrate the group or encourage negativity. How much a person is in charge of her attitudes, her view of things, and her reality also impacts the capacity to sustain oneself. If people aren't centered while in the chaos, they will actually feed it.

From your work with women religious, do you see anything emerging from the chaos of these times that would be worthwhile to note?

There is a goodness and a deep desire to be a transformative presence growing within women religious as they seek to be about mission and their charism in this broken world. I see:

◆ A deep sense of presence, contemplation, and spirituality
◆ A consciousness that has the capacity for healing the environment and a very broken world
◆ A de-centering that is calling women religious to step aside from places of professional leadership to allow a new generation to lead; maybe it is realizing

that they aren't going to be the ones to shape the new reality emerging before us as a world, but they can be the wisdom figures, the guides, and influencers for the next generation

♦ A breathtaking generativity in provinces, congregations, and monastic communities as they move to a more open, global system

♦ A movement toward deeper relationships and communion with one another

And, truth be told, I see many women religious who are not choosing this path or way of being. And this is why the "razor edge" is such a great image. It depicts the danger of not changing and not evolving with the world around them and in not making relevant that which is of essence in their lifestyle.

What qualities do you think leaders need to try to develop that would be helpful for leading in a time of great uncertainty?

♦ Leaders need to strengthen their capacity to trust their "seeing," and their "knowing," that is, naming and acting on what is of the essence instead of wading through tons of data with no action. We have way too much information with too little meaning-making.

♦ Leaders need to look for what is changing in and around them. Where is movement happening? Often we can find this in art, music, poetry, symbolism, science, and business. The arts are well received by women religious. There is a struggle to see the insight and wisdom is some areas of science and business.

♦ Leaders need to ask questions. It is key not to ask the usual or the expected questions.

♦ Leaders need to challenge themselves not to focus on the predictable, the evident questions, but rather to find the unexpected.

- Leaders need to listen deeply and with an empathic heart to see what is, to see what is outside of themselves and what is emerging.
- Leaders need to watch for change. It can come from unexpected places and from unrelated objects or topics being seen together. Our tendency is to focus on the evident. We need to look to the periphery where change is happening, where life is, and let that inform us as to where to go.
- Leaders need to recognize that the next generation of sisters and laity comes from a different perspective than their generation or the majority of sisters. The next generation has a different understanding of global and social issues, of the impact technology is having on the landscape of spirituality and on relationships with the world. The issues from the 1960s and '70s, while similar to those of today, have morphed into problems reflective of today's reality—issues of agribusiness, genetic engineering, and more.
- Leaders need to be aware of the context surrounding their congregation and bring insight and change into the congregation so it can navigate the context or world in which it resides with authenticity and relevance.

Leaders, really all of us, need to "Step out of the traffic! Take a long, loving look at me, your High God, above politics, above everything" (Ps 46:10, translation from *The Message*, by Eugene Peterson). They need to step out of their busyness—go up on the balcony and sit in the place of mystery and grace and see what is transpiring and notice how God is working within them and those they serve.

Women religious talk about wanting to find new ways of being, and not necessarily new ways of doing. What would you recommend to persons desiring to be stretched toward these new ways?

How can women religious today best stay open during these chaotic times to a call to something new within themselves?

Connection with others is critical. Women religious need to move out of their place of isolation, to move from being a closed system to being a more open system where they can let in other viewpoints and people from other walks of life to help them see their lives with fresh eyes.

They need to travel lightly. Women religious are encumbered with multiple responsibilities: those of their congregation, sponsored ministries, families, and professions, and at the same time must deal with often unrealistic expectations from the broader world and church. They need to be compassionate with themselves and one another, allowing themselves to know "enoughness."

Julie Cameron, a writer and artist, encourages individuals to do something different each month, to go some place out of the norm to see different colors, textures, other realities, and to experience something new. I think we all need to be about this. We need to place ourselves in situations that will disturb the familiar, where the deepest "you" has to show up.

I would recommend letting go of perfectionism and fear of failure, and I would encourage people to experiment, learn, refine, and create what is meant to be born.

What would you recommend for leaders who want to tap into the deepest, best, and most creative parts of their congregations?

You can't play to the whole. You have to listen deeply to where the Spirit is calling your congregation and religious life and put that forth fully knowing not everyone will agree. I would recommend that leaders:

- ◆ Go to the places within your congregation of most potential where there is passion, consciousness, and insight and invite those members and associates to work for the good of the whole. Too often leaders are caught in the "tyranny of inclusion" (a tendency to believe that the inclusion of all voices is always necessary in a group's decision-making) and don't allow themselves to call forth those who can further a concept or dream for the sake of the whole.

♦ Invite members to be about more. As leaders it is critical to see the potential, yearnings, and goodness within your members and help them unleash their potential. Leaders need to challenge their members to see and act on their talents and capacities.

♦ Provide "what ifs." Often people can't see possibilities, but once they see the challenge or the shared idea, they respond.

Without a doubt, women religious need to listen to their newer members, younger members, and connect with young people in multiple ways to help them see how to make the depth and essence of the life relevant for these times. Congregations need a breath of fresh air and insight.

If questions can often be more transforming than answers, what kinds of questions do you think would be helpful for women religious leaders to be raising these days—among their members, with their publics, with one another?

♦ Do you know, believe, embrace that first and foremost your commitment is to God? Therefore your relationship to God, your spirituality, and your vowed commitment are absolutely fundamental to living religious life. Are you happy?

♦ What do you need to be freed of so that you can be about mission, be about the Gospel?

♦ What are you willing to risk personally and communally of your finite and precious resources for the life and for mission? In what areas of your life are you willing to be held personally and collectively accountable?

- How will you move beyond congregational boundaries and leverage your collective knowledge, resources, and contacts in order to create a great society; to empower women worldwide; and to bring about social transformation?
- How can you bring together the gift and the grace of the individual and the community to model a new reality for our world and our church that transcends the shadow of individualism and nation-states?
- As a community, what are we "pretending" or "denying" that is keeping us from tapping into our greatest potential as a congregation of women religious today?

13

Reimagining Leadership

Luisa M. Saffiotti

 *Leaders today have the unique challenge of leading through major shifts and transitions. These times require leaders to be innovative, creative, and often daring as they lead groups through experiences of profound decision-making and change. What can assist leaders and help them stay grounded in the midst of turmoil and even danger? To better understand what is needed to reimagine leadership for these times, LCWR invited* **Luisa M. Saffiotti,** *a peace psychologist, clinical psychologist, spiritual director, and retreat director, to reflect on the qualities needed to lead in periods of great uncertainty.*

At the 2007 LCWR assembly, speaker Lynn M. Levo, CSJ, stated that religious life is now in "the nowhere between two somewheres." If this is true, how does it influence any movement forward? How do people live healthily in the in-between time and prepare for moving toward something that is still unclear and unknown?

First there needs to be a consciousness that we are in an in-between time and a willingness to be in that space, as opposed to thinking that we are just at the end of something. There needs to be a willingness to face the questions that an in-between time presents: Who is God at this time? Who is God calling us to be at this time? Who are we called to be as ministers of the Gospel and disciples of Jesus who also have resources, privilege, and voice?

I would also say that there are two primary dimensions to living healthily in an in-between time. The first is to be grounded in a vertical direction, to be grounded in a relationship with God—whatever that means for people—and to be so deeply, deeply connected, anchored, and focused that the relationship profoundly sustains and nourishes the person, and that the person has a sense of partnering with God. The second dimension is to be deeply anchored in the horizontal plane in terms of connectedness and relatedness with others. The quality of this relatedness ideally flows from the vertical relatedness with God. Of course, basic things like self-care and the usual supports needed in a time of transition are also important.

My concern when I look around at people who are in religious life and are really affected by this in-between time is that either or both of these dimensions are not solidly in place. If there is a deep anchoring in God and the support of relatedness with others, then almost anything can happen and we are able to move through it and forward. We hesitate, get stuck, and often move backward when we are not anchored and trusting, or when we have expectations that "it should not be this way," and that if things are difficult it must mean that, particularly as leaders, we are somehow failing, it is somehow our fault. Most often, "it"—the difficulties and turmoil that are naturally part of times of transition—is not the fault of leaders, but it happens easily that members project their own anxieties, frustrations, and even negativity onto leaders, who, if they do not realize that this is what is happening, will get filled up with the negative projections and will feel inadequate and overwhelmed.

Do you have a sense that there's not an awareness that we are in this in-between time, or is it generally accepted?

I think many people accept it, but there are pockets where this is less accepted. I see religious institutes that seem to be more interested in going back to doing things a certain way and recruiting members who will embody an older way of being because that way seems more robust and valuable. There are also parts of the hierarchical structure of the church that affirm and strengthen the older structures and perspectives, despite the changes that are happening. These realities make it even more difficult to be in the in-between space of transition, because to be there in the face of strong pulls toward the older, familiar models and away from the still-unknown newness requires more grounding as well as psychological, spiritual, and human strength. Where there is not this grounding, there can be more regression toward what is familiar and a holding on to it for dear life.

Another factor is that among people being trained for ministry these days, whether for priesthood, religious life, or lay ministry, a large percentage (more than 60 percent of seminarians) are either fairly new to Catholicism or returning after being away for most of their lives. Often they find within Catholicism an identity that they can take on that provides security and comfort. They are very threatened by anything that stretches, broadens, or questions that. They struggle with fully owning the potential of being in an in-between time because it is too scary and overwhelming. Also, because the world at this time is producing more people who psychologically are very fragile and vulnerable, larger numbers of people are coming into ministry this way.

The LCWR assembly was focused on religious life moving into a new frontier. Lynn Levo invited people to think of a frontier as a psychological experience of unlimited possibility, a place where it is easier to be creative, where mistakes are considered new ways of learning. She encouraged people to stop thinking of the decreasing numbers of religious as a disadvantage and rather as chance to be more. What does it take to bring about a shift in thinking like this? How can leaders encourage and assist members to live from this perspective?

Leaders need to bring a real consciousness to the possibility of this shift and need to start modeling it through the language they use and in the way they frame initiatives for their groups. Leaders can promote an alternative way of seeing reality by careful attention to the way things are talked about, because language shapes people's perceptions of what they are going through. Leaders need to be extremely mindful and inten-tional about shaping people's experience of what is going on— be it events or planning for the future—and opening members to a movement in perception so that the idea of a shift seeps into people's consciousness. This is not denial; it is just seeing the reality in a different way.

Leaders need to use themselves as barometers for what their members might also need at this time. If leaders can keep a finger on the pulse of their own experience of trying to shift perspective they will gain valuable input on how to help their members shift perspective. For instance, it is helpful to be aware of stereotypes or assumptions that we may operate from that may not be accurate. Sometimes we think it will be hard-est for the most elderly sisters to shift, when there is a lot of ev-idence that this is not necessarily the case. Sometimes we think we need to protect younger members from some of the realities or we assume that the members in the middle are burnt out with work. It is important to check what assumptions exist and then verify them. My experience with the leaders with whom I work is that at times some of them can get blocked before they even try something different because of anticipating concerns of the members that are not necessarily there.

As religious communities talk about restructuring physical plants and community configurations, perhaps leaders can also restructure some of their own internal thinking and speaking. The external shifts can follow from that internal shift.

It seems as if the kind of shifting called for in religious life today goes beyond incremental change that is somewhat predictable and logi-cal to real and deep transformation, which is often unpredictable and illogical. Do you have a sense that this kind of transformation is being called for in religious life—a transformation that could involve a whole redefinition of who religious are? If so, what would you name as the challenges for leading through a time of deep transformation?

These shifts do at times seem unpredictable and illogical, especially if you think that the harvest is plentiful and laborers are few. What does it mean that fewer people are coming to religious life and more members are getting older? It does seem illogical, but God's logic is not ours. We will get progressively more stuck and frustrated if we keep thinking that things are going to proceed in a way that is logical to us. I find myself using the concept of phase shift, as in chemistry and physics when a substance changes its phase and goes from a gas to a liquid or from a liquid to a solid. That is a profound change that affects the whole identity of the substance.

Do I sense that this is the kind of change being called for in religious life? Yes. We see how the structures of religious life as they have been, with some exceptions, are not working very well anymore. There is a great deal of top heaviness, of institutional structural heaviness, especially in the United States, where the structures fit a time when the numbers were greater and the kinds of ministry were different. Now there seems to be a call for some other kind of presence.

It is really important for leaders to stay very grounded and anchored in their relationship with God, in contemplative listening, to being closely in tune with God. Leaders also need to become deeply aware and conscious of their own areas of resistance to transformation, name them, and understand them so that they do not get in the way.

There are a number of important roles that leaders would want to intentionally assume to help their groups move through deep transformation, and I will name just a few.

- ◆ **Undertaker.** In this role the leader reverently and respectfully puts to rest the realities that have run their course, are no longer viable, and need to be grieved and released.

- *Midwife.* How does a leader attend and alertly assist the birth of new realities, which may well come about in unpredictable and illogical ways? Good midwives are prepared for however the baby needs to be born, particularly since some babies may need creative assistance to see the light.
- *Torchbearer.* How does a leader bear light into places where there is darkness, confusion, or even despair? How does a leader facilitate a deep reprogramming of old habits, attitudes, and customs that can frame reality negatively or keep people in a negative frame—for example, "Oh, we're dying. Oh, we're not going to get any new members."
- *Anchor.* Leaders need to help members name the essential elements of who they are, to help identify and find anchors that allow them to go through whatever happens.
- *Bearer of hope.* This is a hope that imagines the possible in any difficult situation, that trusts that true to God's nature, God is always going to be making something new. How can leaders be a bearer of this kind of hope—tirelessly, gently, but consistently with that message?

Leaders also need to model a spirituality of the *anawim*. Being at home in that spiritual space and trusting that out of the seeming littleness—as seen from the framework of what a congregation's reality was fifty or a hundred years ago—that out of that remnant, God has opted to make something new. If leaders model that spirituality, then this space can be a very exciting one. It could help people to let go and embrace smallness as a place of potential and to catch the excitement of being chosen as a remnant to carry some essential strands of religious life forward and birth something new. I suspect that religious life in the future is not going to be about big numbers and structures but about being pieces of leavening and salt in many places. The challenge is that this is very counterintuitive for what religious life has come to be.

Have you seen any religious institute undergo a process of transformation that has worked well? If so, what were the learnings from that process that others could benefit from hearing?

I haven't seen a whole institute do all of these things, but I've seen different institutes do some of them very meaningfully and very compellingly. The Sisters of Mercy moved their novitiate to Laredo, Texas, which was a conscious move to form women coming in as new members in a more prophetic way. This fits with being small and being remnants, since they are in the minority in a Spanish-speaking context among the poor. The Monroe IHMs' complete overhauling of their motherhouse according to more ecologically safe standards is a witness to the shift in consciousness among religious about the stewardship of creation being part of the work of justice and attending to what is oppressed. There also seems to be a proliferation of initiatives of transforming retreat houses to be more green, raising sustainably produced food, and buying from local farms. Religious communities seem to be at the forefront of attending to the discrepancy that exists between the costs of this kind of agriculture and the lack of access that the most vulnerable people have. There are many groups doing some very intentional restructuring of their administrative structures to be more true to who they want to be. So, while I haven't seen one group that is doing it all, I have seen many groups who are attending to pieces of transformation.

What I have also seen are new communities emerging where there are mixtures of men and women, or lay and religious. The fruits from what we have started to see so far are really powerful. What I do know from those involved in any of these new efforts is that all have required a great deal of effort, energy, creative thinking, and being stretched and pained, and that it has been incredibly exciting for people to see something new come into being.

Another LCWR assembly speaker, John Allen, said that the shifts happening in religious life parallel what is happening in the broader world in these postmodern times. What do you think religious life could learn from the broader world as it lives through this time of significant change? What does religious life do well that might serve as a model or sign of hope for others?

We can talk about both the negative and the positive of these postmodern times and of social and economic globalization. Some of the negatives that we see seem to be driven by fear and anxiety—worrisome protectionist behavior; wanting to maximize one's own gains; resentment toward those who are different and of systems that are different; resistance to seeing structures, governments, economies, and social relations differently. We see this anxiety in the questions being voiced in our society about immigration. As the ground shifts beneath the feet of this society, we see a lot of fears emerging about identity. How will having all these people who look a bit different, speak different languages, and relate in different ways challenge our white Anglo-Saxon and Protestant approach to life? Who then do we become?

Positively, we see growing grassroots movements, indigenous movements, and other groups that are intent on coming together, finding their voice, and emerging as alternatives to mainstream realities and offerings.

All of this parallels what is happening in religious life. There is some fear based on restructuring and concerns about protecting one's own identity. What if we cease to be as we have been? What happens if you throw your lot into a larger pool and become identified with the more broad charism of religious life, rather than with just your own congregation's charism? So you see some of the fear, but you also see the creativity and fertility. Often the most creative life-giving initiatives within religious communities are coming not from leadership, but from somewhere else. This is consistent with organic growth, which has to come from inside the Earth.

Religious life is at its best and is prophetic when it has been able to be free enough to let go of structures that are no longer allowing it to stand firm and tall, but rather are actually constraining it and binding it in some way. Religious life at its best dares to see reality clearly and dares to speak the truths about it and speak them to power. Religious life at its best ventures to the margins to see the reality from there and brings that vision back toward the center to transform and renew it.

It is also really crucial at this time to consider religious life as sacrament, as a sign pointing toward liberation and full humanity for all God's people. If religious life commits to taking that kind of prophetic stance, being on the margins, seeing reality from there, and being ferment for change by speaking of these realities, then it can be a model for the world. In these postmodern times there is so much opportunity, but also so much confusion, disorientation, fear, and retrenching because of trying to hold on to some sense of stability. Religious life can model the courage that is needed to recognize that one's identity may not be in the same place it was in the past and to point to where it really is now. Anthropology tells us that these kinds of shifts happen without having to be planned and systematic, and that this is how groups pull society along through changes.

Margaret Wheatley says that living systems change when some part of the system notices something, chooses to be disturbed by it, and shares the information with the rest of the system. Would you say that this pattern of change is true in religious institutes?

It can be the pattern, but I don't think it always is. A lot depends on how much openness there is in a system to seeing clearly and to being disturbed by what one sees. Some religious institutes have potentially a lot to lose if they choose to be disturbed. Groups that have large works, such as hospitals and universities that are doing a lot of good, may find it harder to be disturbed by calls to other ways of being present. I would hesitate to say that this is the pattern for change, but it often can be what brings about change. It would be the same as taking an organism with a very, very tough hide, like dinosaur hide. If you brush the organism with a feather, it is not even going to notice. This organism needs prodding, and probably with a spear, before it will notice anything. Other organisms are so sensitive that a feather would be major stimulus. You also have to look at a system's past and its historical memory. How much protective armor did the group have to create because of its history?

Margaret Wheatley also says that only when this disturbing information becomes so important that the system cannot deal with it in its present state will the system begin to change; she adds that the system must let go and live in uncertainty before it can reorganize in a new way and with new meaning. Would you say that this will be the case for religious life?

Definitely. There are systems already there, and they are very sensitive and are already adjusting. Others will get to a point where they will have no other choice but to attend to the information, and they will transform more slowly or they will cease to be in their current form because they have run their course. There are so many religious institutes in the world. There must have been many inspired founders in the middle of the nineteenth century and quite a few of the institutes that they founded seem to be winding down. They were formed to meet a specific need of specific populations, and those needs are now being taken care of by civil society or by others. This is not typically true of the big orders that have been around for centuries, but rather for many smaller, regional groups. In these cases, the disturbance comes when there is no need any more for what they have been doing, so either they start to do something else or they cease to exist.

We should note that the response to a disturbance can go in two directions, and we are seeing this in the church and in religious life right now. We can look upon the changing social mores and changes in the ways that people relate to one another and see that as a disturbance for the church. It can disturb the church toward opening—opening to noticing these realities, noticing people's needs, noticing who needs to be embraced and welcomed. Because these realities can also generate anxiety and fear, they can also move the church toward closing or pushing away and withdrawing. It's like when you touch the tail of an animal it does one thing; if you touch its ears it does something else. You have to be careful not to assume that a disturbance will produce one type of change in a system. And what happens in a system that tries to hold both responses simultaneously? So, I think that responses to a disturbance are definitely going to happen, and in some cases are already happening, and they can be complex.

If it is true that we choose what disturbs us, that we notice what is meaningful to us, what can leaders learn from this? How can leaders invite members into change processes if members are not feeling that change is necessary or that the matters at hand are of importance to them?

I would go back to the idea of seeing. Leaders need to model seeing clearly, as well as very non-judgmentally, in order to help membership notice what it sees. This is assuming that leaders are willing to see clearly and broadly, which sometimes by virtue of being in their role is hard. Sometimes the closer you get to the top of the leadership pyramid, the more the role prevents you from being in touch with certain things. Even when an institution is on the threshold of change, there can be a form of what Jon Sobrino calls "culpable blindness," where a person chooses not to see because the implicstions of seeing clearly would be very inconvenient. Then you have to wonder whether not seeing becomes a block to the action of the Holy Spirit. This brings us to the brink of whether we really believe that God is God, that the Spirit does make things new and that, as difficult as things may be, we will not be dropped midstream. It involves inviting people to a radical, essential act of faith.

Psychological development can also be an obstacle to seeing and thus being disturbed. There are some things that we need to grow into the capacity to see and, when there is not sufficient maturity either individually or collectively, we won't have the capacity to see or respond to. There is also always a cost to seeing fully, and that is hard, both communally and individually.

Ken Wilber talks about how systems are nested, so that whatever happens at one level of the system will invariably be reflected upward and downward through the system. To the extent that leaders can do their own necessary work to notice their own resistances and obstacles to seeing and thus become more and more able to see, then the likelihood of the whole system or institution seeing clearly increases. Similarly, when leadership cannot seem to see and act consequentially, but the grassroots membership does start to see, then that seeing inevitably also trickles upward through the system.

What kinds of supports do religious congregation members need as they live through change? What can leaders provide to members? What kinds of supports do leaders need?

The vertical and horizontal dimensions are both essential—a deep spiritual groundedness with God, whatever that means for people, and communal relatedness. There also needs to be a distilling of the core elements of the charism of a group, so that what is essential gets carried along. There needs to be a holding of the essential, as well as openness to expanding it to include the notion of a charism of religious life as a whole. Also, leaders can support their members with a real attentiveness to the language, the discourse, the ritual, and how they themselves relate to a new consciousness. This helps members because they feel like their whole system is moving together in a certain direction.

Leaders themselves need to be supported by a lot of dialogue with other leaders, perhaps with some input or facilitation to process how they are experiencing being in their role at this time. They could also be helped by taking up some real consciousness of their role, as leaders generally, but also as leaders in times of transition in particular, and the price that exacts. If leaders are realistic with themselves about this, then they will be better able to take care of themselves in it and be aware of their individual and collective vulnerabilities. It is harder to lead through times of uncertainty and transition.

It is important also to get support when there are difficulties within leadership teams. If you have a "dysfunctional" or troubled leadership team, it's going be much harder for that team to effectively lead the whole group through transition, and it is going to be even harder for the designated leader, whether a provincial or congregational leader, to do what she needs to do. In my work with some leadership teams, the first order of business had to be to sort out the dynamics around the places of real struggle within the team.

Is there anything you would like to add?

I think it would be valuable if leaders could find themselves embracing, maybe even with excitement, the sense that being a leader right now is a whole new enterprise. Leaders don't have to simply reproduce what they have seen in other leaders. It could be helpful if leaders could see this as a time like Lynn Levo described—a time of being at a new frontier, where

it is okay to make mistakes because mistakes are ways of learning. Leaders are not going to lead perfectly though transitions.
If the whole enterprise of religious life is being redefined, then
it makes sense that leadership is also being redefined.

In the midst of this, it is important for leaders to stay anchored and be deeply conscious of what they are modeling for
those who are following. Leaders need followers. It is like
climbing a mountain or making tracks in the wilderness.
Leaders are going and others are following. Sometimes they
will go off on the side and realize that they have hit a dead
end and will have to go back, and that is okay. Leaders just
need to remember that they are modeling a way for their
members to follow.

14

Leading through a Time of Change

Ray Dlugos, OSA

 *In the shifting sands of organizational life today, almost all leaders are faced with the challenge of helping their organization navigate significant experiences of change. LCWR engaged psychologist* **Ray Dlugos, OSA**, *to speak on the dynamics of and normal responses to change and offer insights and suggestions on how leaders might best work with their organizations in coping with these realities for the good of all. Father Ray served on the staff and later as chief executive officer of The Southdown Institute before becoming vice president of mission and ministry at Merrimack College.*

At this year's LCWR assembly, the keynoter, Laurie Brink, OP, spoke of "the elephant in the living room" of religious congregations today. She named the elephant "indecision," noting that religious congregations are not moving together in any direction, and suggested that unless congregations choose a common direction and move together, religious life will not survive. From your experience, would you say that this is true? And, if so, what might be happening that has led to this phenomenon within religious communities?

I would agree that we seem to be paralyzed in our ability to make a decision to go forward in any particular direction. I think what is underneath that indecision is an inner experience of real ambivalence—an ambivalence that arises from a sense of powerlessness or futility. It's often expressed as, "Nothing that we do is going to make any difference anyway, so why should we even bother?" Or, "Absolutely, something should be done, something should change, somebody should do something different, but that somebody is somebody other than me." We often think that if only other people would change, then everything would be all right, and allow ourselves the luxury of waiting for the world outside of us to change before we take any steps ourselves.

If we are going to move forward, we have to name the reality of our ambivalence and challenge it. Ambivalence looks for a place that is comfortable where it can just sit. We can challenge ambivalence in ourselves and others by raising rather than lowering expectations, which will inevitably evoke a reaction of greater resistance. The raising of expectations shakes us out of the comfort of staying still, but in a way that is disturbing, and so our reaction to raised expectations is usually not positive or cooperative. If we are going to overcome the ambivalence that is paralyzing us, we need to withstand the initial resistance to doing anything new or different, absorb the initial reactivity that will come with a fury, and continue to expect more of ourselves and one another rather than less. However, while we need to raise expectations, it is essential that we communicate those raised expectations in a manner that is not judgmental or demanding. In the face of condemnation and demands, ambivalence grows stronger and causes us to dig our heels in even deeper. The raising of expectations has to be accompanied by a lot of love and reassurance that makes it possible for us and others to go forward with some security.

Two mistakes that leaders could make are to pull back on their affection, which only makes members sink lower into their ambivalence, or to lower their expectations of members in hope that members will at least do something. Neither of these approaches can overcome ambivalence.

Do you think, in general, that leaders have lowered their expectations of members?

I think so. The inevitable forces that occur within the dynamics of any group are such that group members collude to disempower the leader, and we have successfully disempowered the leadership of religious communities to the point that leaders are afraid to call members to more than what we are willing to do voluntarily. We have put leaders in boxes where they can only do what we want them to do rather than what they are called to do. Men and women do that a little differently, but we both do it. Leaders respond to their fear of being viewed as too authoritarian by lowering their expectations of members. However, it is important to distinguish challenging people in a stance of harshness from calling people to something greater and higher through a relationship of affection.

Is there any particular area of religious life where you believe expectations should be raised?

I think there are several. We need to look at all the essential elements of religious life, such as living the life of the Gospel based on the evangelical counsels, living the common life, giving love and service to others, and being a prophetic witness to God's presence in this moment in history. What I see happening is that each one of us may be strongly attracted to and experience a deep sense of call to some of those aspects but not necessarily all of them. We would like to have the piece of religious life that is attractive to us and consistent with our strengths be the defining aspect of religious life, while paying lip service to or minimizing the importance of the others. For example, someone may be very deeply committed to ministry and service to others and open to being challenged to stretch and grow and go deeper and deeper in this area of his or her life. But, at the same time, he or she might have a strong resistance to the common life, to being part of the whole, to having to rub elbows and go forward with plans that may not quite mesh with their own but are for the common good.

So, if religious life is going to become a truly life-giving experience for the people living it, expectations need to be raised for each of us in the places where we are most resistant to having expectations raised. This requires a real willingness to challenge ourselves. Leaders have a role in inviting us to do this. To move religious life forward, each one of us has to look at what it is about this life that I don't really buy into and I'm not that interested in and then ask how I might be called to conversion in that area.

Religious life today seems to require a capacity to live with change as a continuous experience. What could help religious live healthily in this kind of environment?

Life, and not just religious life, requires a capacity to live with change as a continuous experience, and I don't think that's just today, I think that's life. Life on this planet has always been a constant evolution into something different and new. The social forces in organizations are always in upheaval, the economic forces that drive us are always shifting and changing—even the physical climate is changing. We are all, as people, living in an environment where forces are changing all around us. We have to find a way to respond to them.

I think religious have a real role to play in terms of figuring out how to be in a reality that is changing all the time and isn't under our control and entering into it with faith, hope, and love, rather than from a stance of mere survival. We are called to be people who genuinely search for God in the midst of the changing reality. From our religious traditions, charisms, and spirituality, we have the resources that make us better educated than any other group on the planet to live with and respond effectively to change. We have the spiritualities that call us all to detachment in some form and that invite us to be ready and able to serve the evolving needs of the world. If we are going to respond to this ever-changing world in the healthiest way for ourselves and in service to the world, we have to look at the reality of the world without any denial or illusion, and without pretending that the changes are not also happening to us.

We also need to resist our innate desire to react to change. We have to allow the experiences of change to rattle around inside of us and pay attention to what they are doing to us as individual human beings and as a group of human beings. That means needing to talk about how the change feels, whether it frightens me, makes me angry, is a source of sadness and grief. We need to be honest about how things are actually affecting us and using that honesty to see truths about ourselves. Seeing the truth is not usually very fun because it makes us pretty vulnerable. But it is in this very contemplative listening space that we can see the changes that are happening as an invitation to the place where we really encounter God—which is the point of religious life. The key to doing this well is found not only in praying well, but in praying in a way that allows us to tell the truth about what is happening in our lives and the truth about ourselves. And that is hard.

Is there anything that you could recommend to leaders who might want to encourage that kind of honest appraisal of reality among their members?

I think they could start by telling the truth as fully as possible about what is really happening and not try to protect members from the financial realities, personnel realities, and other pragmatic realities. And then they could call each member to be responsible for this truth. But they also need to engage people with this information on an emotional level. I think some leaders are doing this, but I don't know if we do it long enough or regularly enough, or stay with our feeling level long enough to have it be really revelatory. We need to invite people to acknowledge their fear, their anger, and certainly their sadness and grief over what we are losing, because change is about loss. You don't change anything without losing something, even if you are getting something more. We need to name our anger and not have it be about what is happening outside of us, but letting it reveal our neediness and our powerlessness. As events are happening in religious communities, we need to give members the time, space, permission, and guidance to go into their own emotional life and see what it is really revealing about themselves.

In some situations of reconfiguration, I have seen communities work hard at engaging members in making collaborative decisions, and they are doing a great job. But I don't know if we always acknowledge the loss that these kinds of change involve. The emphasis seems to be that this new move will be a good thing for us as we go forward, that it will help us do new and better things and do them longer. That all is probably absolutely true, but when members start to feel that they are losing something and if that loss is not addressed, then their hearts and minds will not be engaged in embracing the new reality. Telling the truth in these situations means that we have to be straightforward and honest about the costs and the loss. And, of course, we often don't know what it is that we are going to lose until we actually start losing it.

What about voluntary change? What leads people to choose to change on their own?

This is a very tricky question because unless we have to change, we tend not to. Rarely do we choose to change. Even when my head knows that a change would be good, it takes a lot of convincing of the rest of me to take the steps to change.

People in religious life see that this life, as it is now, will not last. But when we see that, we tend to think that someone else has to do something about it, rather than that I have to do something. Change generally has to be seen as something that will be in our best interest, that it will benefit us more than it will cost us.

This is where religious are called to approach change differently from most people and go into it with a sense of faith, rather than a focus on the practicalities. In religious life we probably are not going to see how change will benefit us. Some of the changes that we are going to be called to in the future are not going to be seen as benefiting us at all. They are going to cost a great deal, and we are going to lose a lot through them. So, the resistance is going to be very powerful. If we pretend that change is not going to cost us, then as soon as it does, we will go back to the way we were before.

Responding to change requires that people be on their toes, yet we often prefer to settle. The biggest challenge of change is the work of maintaining it. So, leaders are the ones who are going to have to exert the energy needed to make sure that people stay the course of change. Things will get difficult and will get hard. This is when leaders have to keep the attention of the members on why changes are important and necessary. They are going to have to do lots of engaging with resistance, and they are going to need to do it with great affection and love. The inertia of ambivalence is very powerful and it will keep trying to pull us back.

At the LCWR assembly, Lynn Levo, CSJ, raised the questions: "Are our boundaries as religious institutes too porous? Do we need to name more clearly who we are as religious?" How important is it for religious today to be clear on what religious life is?

We deal with a healthy and creative tension in trying to keep a balance between wanting to be part of the rest of the human race and needing to have an identity of our own. The danger is that we can try to resolve that tension prematurely by saying that we want to go one way at the exclusion of the other. We can say that we want to include everyone with us, that we don't want to be set apart from the human race and want to be joined with them completely. And we absolutely need to attend to that desire within us. If we separate ourselves completely, though, then we are not of use to anybody. But we do need to see ourselves as set apart from others and acknowledge, without condescension or superiority, that we are not like the rest of people. Both truths about our identity need to be held in a creative tension, not giving into one or the other prematurely, if we are to find our true identity as religious. Living with an awareness of these two poles is a tense place, but I think that our vocation is precisely to be in that very tense place, and to be there with depth.

Religious life does set us apart in terms of what we are called to be. Our uniqueness is going to be in our willingness to go deeper in the way we respond to the reality of life happening to us along with everyone else. It is not particularly useful to set ourselves apart from others in surface ways like dressing differently or living in different kinds of houses unless that really serves the deeper project of engaging the real experiences of life in a deeper and different way from that of most people. The unique identity of religious is in the depth by which we embrace life and other people.

Can you say more about the depth with which you believe religious are called to live?

I think this is found primarily in the difference between reacting to things happening to us, to external events crashing into us, and responding to whatever is happening with a genuine sense of faith, hope, and love. Going deeper means not succumbing to the illusions that we are safe from harm and not vulnerable because of the security we might enjoy as people with education, influence, and even financial security, but deliberately seeing the precariousness of our existence and our powerlessness to control those forces that make us vulnerable. Going deeper means finding the grace that is found when in weakness, power reaches perfection.

Going deeper means a willingness to risk—rather than attempt to mitigate all risk to ourselves—while maximizing the safety of others in our care. Going deeper means to risk humiliation and rejection by offering our service when it is not the service requested by the world and even the church, but it is what we genuinely and authentically have to offer. Going deeper means having the humility to learn from the least of our brothers and sisters as well as the most of our brothers and sisters and the courage and willingness to teach both. Going deeper means allowing the various points of view and perspectives so widely available in this post-post-postmodern world, including and especially those with which we do not agree and seem to be dismissive of our own perspective, to have an impact on us and perhaps challenge us. Going deeper means opening ourselves to criticism as a valuable resource to self-awareness rather than defensively protecting what we have settled into as a way to engage life comfortably. To pick up a point I tried to make earlier, going deeper means attending especially to the invitations to change to which I may be most resistant and being self-critical enough to look at why I am resisting those changes.

During my first year studying theology at the Washington Theological Union, Ed Dobbin, OSA, taught us about the transcendental method of the Canadian Jesuit Bernard Lonergan. That method has four steps, and those four steps challenge us to go deeper in exactly the way I think we need to. We are called to pay close attention to what is really happening to us; to be curious and ask a lot of questions about our experience in order to see it as fully and as accurately as possible;

to be critical, especially self-critical about the responses we see ourselves and others automatically considering as the best ways to respond; and finally to act in the most responsible way possible. I think we are called to this depth in the smallest and most insignificant experiences as well as in experiences that seem to be cosmic and universal. I think all of the charisms and traditions of religious life show us different ways to do this, different ways of being called to engage intentionally in this kind of depth in as many experiences of life as we can.

There are many external forces trying to shape religious life today that may try to define our unique vocation in other ways. How can group members engage these forces in a meaningful way and in a way that helps them be clear about who they are and who they want to be?

There are lots of forces—the institutional church, the laity, and all sorts of other forces—that want religious to be what they want us to be. If we put a real check on our reactivity to this, we can respond in a way that is very healthy and whole. For example, we might read some directive from the Vatican about religious life and find our muscles tensing and the hairs on the back of our neck standing up. We start saying, "They have no right to talk to us like that. Who do they think they are?"

I suggest that rather than just react, we might be more consistent with who we are called to be if we can receive the efforts of any external force, whether it is the institutional church or the secular world, without dismissing them too quickly or submitting to them unreflectively. We receive the message with an authentic desire to listen to it, to consider what wisdom that voice might contain that we would not otherwise have access to. Instead of pushing that external voice aside and reacting to it by dismissing it, we can bring it into our contemplative space and ask: "How does this rattle inside of me? What in this might really be calling me forth to something deeper and more authentic?" If we could do that, we are going to be in a place that is a lot less dismissive of people, which is a natural, but very violent, tendency born of our innate drive for self-preservation. Instead, we allow for the possibility that there might be wisdom contained in what others are asking of us that we would never ask of ourselves.

All of these external forces that try to define us have something to say. We do need to figure out what we are called to, because we are not called to be everything that everyone wants us to be, but we can't do what we need to do if we dismiss input coming to us just because it might be coming from sources we have already learned to mistrust. Otherwise, we are just talking to ourselves. We need to listen to what we feel when we hear the input, and know that those feelings are more revelatory of ourselves than of the external force calling us to something. We need to listen to the voice of God in the midst of all those voices and forces. With all of that input, we make a choice that is consistent with our integrity as persons and with our vocation and mission.

You have said that you think religious life in the future will include martyrdom. What makes you say this, and what would you say to leaders in particular about this?

What we witnessed in Myanmar in the fall when the monks took on the secular, oppressive government was very powerful. That has something to say to us as religious. I don't think that we are all called to put ourselves in front of machine guns and let people kill us, but there are all sorts of martyrdoms in life. The willingness to surrender things that matter to us for the sake of what we are called to is a form of martyrdom. It is martyrdom when we allow ourselves to engage our own resistance to different parts of religious life. I might say, "I work very hard for the poor, I have a deep prayer life, and I have a very simple lifestyle, but I can't stand living with those in my community and I want to be by myself." Perhaps the martyrdom that I choose is to enter into the common life so that I am authentic to my call. These are the kinds of martyrdoms that will come when we allow ourselves to be called to do what we resist because it is going to be very inconvenient and filled with loss for us. There is also the martyrdom of trying to break away and free ourselves from the unjust, violent, and non-life-giving forces within our culture and society. If we are not willing to accept this kind of martyrdom, then there is not much point in religious life.

Often leaders say that they know that there needs to be a shift in the concept of religious life leadership today, but they don't know how to bring that shift about. What do you believe leaders could do to help bring the members along in changing the concept of leadership in religious life?

What I understand of the dynamics of leadership I have learned from being a group therapist, which is a lot simpler than trying to lead a congregation of several hundred men or women. But I do think that it helps to have an awareness and understanding of the dynamics that occur between people who are in positions of authority and the people they are trying to lead. While leaders have a job description and a mission that are probably outlined in constitutions and congregational documents and based on the Gospel, the reality is that every individual member has his or her own job description for the leader. Each one of us wants our leader to do something for us and to take care of us in a way that we want to be taken care of. My job description for my leader is, "Leave me alone. Take care of everybody else—particularly those who are bothering me—but leave me alone to do what I want." Other people have very different ideas. Some want to be more dependent on the leader, have their leader present with them, receive more attention. If leaders tried to match the expectations and meet the needs of every single member, they would fail. They would burn out and, in the end, no one would be challenged to grow.

Often the last thing we want leaders to do is to call us forth to fidelity to our very difficult and painful mission, which is just the sort of calling forth to change that we have been talking about here. When leaders take their eye off the ball and start assuming that their job is to respond to the individual needs of members, then they won't be doing their real job, which is to call forth members into mission. Yet when they try to do that, they will encounter enormous resistance of all kinds. People try to disempower the leader in all kinds of ways, and this needs to be named. I think if leaders can be better educated on the natural dynamics that occur when human beings are gathered in groups, and particularly on what happens between members and the person of authority, it will be helpful. There are ways to respond to these dynamics, and learning these ways can help people carry out their leadership rather than be disempowered by the members.

Is there anything that we didn't talk about today that you might want to say to leaders?

Being a leader is a very, very stressful thing. My observation is that the time when religious are called to make real sacrifices for the sake of the community is when they are called to leadership. Often, in order to serve their brothers and sisters, these religious are called to surrender ministries that they deeply love and in which they are very effective. That's a tremendous sacrifice. I have met and been edified by leaders who recognize that sacrifice and have allowed the martyrdom that it exacts to be a deep, faith-filled, and transformative experience for them.

I would like to suggest that leaders take the transformation that has happened to them in accepting this sacrificial change in their lives and use it as a model for what they can call members to. One of the realizations that I have come to is that the point of religious life is not what I can do for others, although I am called to that. But what is essential is what religious life does to me and the conversion and transformation it exacts. Often what most shapes and forms us are the things in life that we most resist, whether that be in the living of the vows, the common life, or ministry. The places of resistance are so sacred. If we resolve the tension that we feel in them too easily, then we are missing most of what religious life can do for us.

15

Adaptive Leadership

Marty Linsky

 **Marty Linsky** *is a prominent thinker in the field of adaptive leadership, a way of leading that helps accomplish deep change. Adaptive leaders learn to thrive in complex, challenging settings, and empower their organizations to respond to challenges courageously and creatively.*

A professor at Harvard's Kennedy School for more than twenty-five years, Mr. Linsky is a co-founder of the Cambridge Leadership Associates and a co-author of ten books, including Leadership on the Line *and* The Practice of Adaptive Leadership. *He also served as chief secretary and counselor to Massachusetts Governor Bill Weld; assistant director at Harvard's Institute of Politics; executive editor of "The Advocates" on PBS; editorial writer and reporter,* The Boston Globe; *assistant minority leader of the Massachusetts House of Representatives; and Massachusetts assistant attorney general.*

You speak about the lure of the status quo, noting that the creative and successful responses organizations have made in the past to challenges can prevent those organizations from adapting and thriving in a new context as conditions in the present change. In initiating a new process for moving into the future, LCWR seems to be indicating that it knows the status quo no longer serves. Can you speak more about how an organization comes to recognize

*the limitations of the status quo and begins to acknowledge a need
for more deep change?*

Our experience is that there is so much of a commitment invested in the status quo in organizational life that it takes an
outside pressure to dislodge that stability. In the private-sector
world, the pressure for change may come through a challenge
to do or produce something different. In the non-profit world,
it may come from diminished resources. In the case of
Catholic sisters, it may also come from a lack of new human
resources coming to your communities, and perhaps from a
feeling that your life is becoming less and less relevant. From
knowing a little of your story in recent years, it seems that another creator of pressure could be the tension that exists between what Catholic sisters name as their highest priorities
and what the broader organization you work within (the
Catholic Church) names for you. It also sounds as if Catholic
sisters are finding yourselves in a position where you are trying
to challenge and modify some of those expectations. All of
those kinds of pressures begin to give people the will and the
courage to move off the status quo.

*You acknowledge how tempting it is to deal with adaptive changes
as though they were technical challenges that could be solved out
of former ways of thinking and acting. Catholic sisters are at a
place now of wanting to go forward differently and having to do
so in the midst of many unknowns as well as with the ambiguity of
moving forward in ways that may not have any precedent. What
could you say to us about leading in ways that are unfamiliar and
may have to be figured out by trial and error?*

Our own experience and observation is that when you are beginning to initiate change it is useful to bring what we call an
experimental mindset to that process. Thinking of yourself as
running experiments rather than solving problems enables you
to do numerous things.

One is that you can run multiple experiments at the same time. You don't have to put all your eggs in one basket. Second is that when you think of yourself as running an experiment then the lack of success is not seen as failure, but rather as a learning opportunity. You are stepping into a place where you have never been before, and the kind of anxiety that produces is perfectly normal and understandable. But when you are thinking of running an experiment, you have a mindset of openness to trying several different things. Then you shift your emphasis to close monitoring of the experiments and of even considering midcourse directional changes. In other words, you bring a whole different kind of spirit to the work.

We think of a vision or strategic plan as someone's or some group's best guess at a moment in time. What can cause much difficulty is when organizations commit to a single course and stick to it even though the data suggest that the course isn't the right way. So, visions and strategic plans shouldn't be used as documents that will determine how an organization will go forward. What is a more useful frame is to think of yourself as being in the business of inventing the future and running a bunch of experiments to see what will work.

LCWR is leading its members through a five-year contemplative process of continuously and deliberately stepping back to look at the needs of the world as well as the realities of our lives from the long view in order to discern what the world most needs of Catholic sisters today. This is similar to what you term getting off the dance floor and taking "the balcony view." Can you speak more about why the balcony view is particularly important in this age of fast-paced living? What can be done from the balcony that cannot be done from the dance floor?

Taking the balcony view and stepping back and seeing the bigger picture enables you to be more realistic because you see patterns that are not always visible in the day-to-day pressure under which we work. When you are able to stand back and see what is really going on, you can reorder your priorities and values as a result and then step back into the fray with more confidence and a clearer sense of purpose.

Our experience is that people don't always want leaders to get up in the balcony very much because they are happy with the leaders being preoccupied with whatever it is they want the leaders to be preoccupied with. This seems to be what has happened with Catholic sisters within the organization of the church. You have stood back, looked at what's really going on in the world, and said here is where our contributions ought to be. That kind of stance generates exactly the kind of disruption Catholic sisters have experienced. So you have actually demonstrated exactly what we say about taking the balcony view—that it is both extremely useful and extremely provocative, especially in organizations where people, or at least some factions, are happy with the way things are.

The LCWR contemplative process stresses the importance of listening to one another's insights about where religious life is being invited to move. You say that the greater a leader's capacity to orchestrate multiple interpretations of an organization's challenge, the more likely the organization is to produce innovative insights. Can you say more about the challenges of orchestrating the interpretations of an organization's members and the roles of dissonance and consonance in creating harmony?

Our experience is that when you're inventing the future and searching for *next* practices rather than looking for *best* practices, the more voices that you can bring to bear in that conversation, the more likely it is that you will be able to generate ideas and options that will be both accepted broadly and deeply and will get you where you want to go. The danger is the wider or broader the conversation, the more likely it is to come out differently from the destination that you originally envisioned. However, the advantage is that you will open up more creative ideas and you will have a greater commitment to the outcome, whatever the outcome is, than you would have had otherwise.

For example, your organization and the various religious communities could generate multiple interpretations of what is going on for Catholic sisters today. You could ask: What is our particular role at this moment in history? What is our unique contribution in saving the world? As you do so, you are going to challenge a lot of people's views of what is going on and how the world works. If you can create the kind of holding environment that can keep people feeling safe as you undertake that process, it can be an enormously productive process that will generate possibilities that are literally beyond people's imaginations.

Your recommendations for helping an organization successfully adapt and thrive include institutionalizing reflection and continuous learning and seeking out new ideas from disciplines other than one's own. Can you speak to some of the challenges to doing this in our action-oriented, outcome-focused environment?

I think we have to recognize that the work of deep change for an organization is demanding and that some people just won't make it through. In organizations that are facing such change, there is a need for a willingness to say implicitly to those folks who don't have the energy any more to engage in the hard work of study and learning: We can't afford to risk the future to make you feel comfortable. The issue then becomes not one of ignoring those members, but of taking responsibility for the fact that your commitment to the ongoing community may actually leave them behind.

Paying attention to this and taking responsibility for it will not only be the right thing to do from a humane perspective, but it will be the right thing to do from a political perspective. For example, your members who will be engaged in the work of adapting and learning will be energized by that kind of activity. But they will not want to see their colleagues who are not able to join in that kind of activity treated badly. So the challenge for the leader is to pay attention to those unable to participate in change, be empathetic and caring toward them, and let them live the rest of their lives as comfortably as possible, without expectations that their desires become the center of the community. That will not only be the right thing to do for them, but it will also give an important signal to others about what is required to go into the future in a viable way.

Is there anything else you would want to say to women religious leaders at this time?

I think the challenges you have before you are absolutely fascinating and really important. Leading communities through these very complicated transitions is critical work, but doing so will assure that the service you offer in a changing and different world remains relevant. I wish you all well in those endeavors.

LEADING IN DIFFICULT TIMES

16

Leading in the Midst of Polarization

Andra Medea

 **Andra Medea** *is a writer, project developer, and theorist on issues of conflict and violence, specifically, crisis prevention. The author of* Conflict Unraveled, *she taught conflict management at Northwestern University and the University of Chicago.*

Recognizing the growing tendency toward polarization in society today, LCWR sought an interview with Andra to explore the causes of polarization and the unique challenges and opportunities those in leadership positions have when they find themselves in a polarized situation. What could we learn about leading effectively when faced with polarization? What might help us be more effective leaders? Is there anything in the history and experience of women religious that might be helpful to share with the wider world about responding non-violently in polarizing situations?

You have been following the situation of LCWR and the Vatican's Congregation for the Doctrine of the Faith. What is it that interested you in this situation?

Many people are watching LCWR right now. You've captured the imagination and the hopes of people who are looking for something more from our leaders—some deeper, gracious voice in these polarized times.

I first started talking with the then–LCWR president Pat Farrell, OSF, after someone sent her a copy of my book, *Conflict Unraveled*. She and the leaders of her LCWR region asked me to develop a workshop called Leadership in Polarized Times. The goal of the workshop was to identify ways of moving past polarization, even in a less than ideal world.

My work is like being a whitewater guide. In the midst of whitewater, everything is boiling white. You can hardly think for the roaring in your ears. But there are markers to watch for. A vertical spray means a boulder: don't go there. Off to one side, perhaps the water kind of shimmers: that's an eddy, calm water. You can go there for a moment's peace and catch your breath.

At first a situation may look like an incomprehensible mess. But once you can pick out the markers, it starts making sense. Then you can map a constructive course.

What happens typically when situations of disagreement become polarized?

Once a situation becomes polarized, all sides split into predictable roles: villains, heroes, or victims. Let's say progressives are villains and conservatives are heroes who need to fight to protect civilization (the victim). Or conservatives are villains and progressives are heroes who fight to protect the planet. Or the Tea Party is the hero, and taxpayers are victims, and poor people are villains. Or the Tea Party is the villain and poor people are victims—you get the idea.

Someone is always a hero, and someone else is the villain. Only the roles keep switching. The hero turns into a villain and becomes victim. Meanwhile, everyone's fighting so much that the real work never gets done.

Virginia Satir was the first to figure this out: the roles keep switching, and there's no way to stop it. There are no brakes on this thing. The problem is the pattern itself, which is destructive, wasteful, and wildly unstable.

This pattern, by the way, makes progress very difficult, and squanders resources. The estimates are that Republicans alone spent half a billion dollars on this last election. Yet when it all blows over, there's very little to show for it. After that hard fought election we have no new solutions, and many critical issues—like climate change and coastal flooding—were never even discussed. Needless to say, this is not what we want from our leaders. But once in the pattern, it's difficult finding a way out.

What role does fear play in creating polarization?

People think polarization is all about the other side being harmful, even evil. It's actually driven by anger and fear. The anger is obvious, but fear is more significant than you'd think. Polarized people feel threatened; they're terrified of what will happen if the other side wins. Being afraid, they fight harder. Wanting to look strong, they attack, which only frightens the first side. So the first side, in turn, fights harder. You'll notice that people don't get frightened and change their minds or get frightened and give up. They get frightened and fight harder. Since you know this is going to happen, you might consider the advantages of not frightening people or embarrassing the other side. After all, losing face is one of the things people fear.

A dignified loss that preserves one's integrity is an entirely different thing. If you think about it, the very concept of dignified loss goes missing in polarized situations. When it does appear, it's stabilizing.

One advantage of women religious is that you tend not to frighten people, and have no desire to embarrass others. You're also not very fearful. It's easier for you to stop, find your footing, and reflect on your choices. You're not as likely to get swept away. That takes courage. It's refreshing.

You can think of polarization as a forest fire, sweeping everything in front of it. Quiet courage is like a firebreak, a fuel-free zone. Fear and anger hit it and lose momentum. Calm, steady courage deprives polarization of the fuel it needs to spread. Deep courage that foregoes anger isn't common in our society. But we admire seeing it in our religious leaders. It's rare and startling; it makes people stop and think.

Of course, courage alone has its limits; you do need a plan. Strategic non-violence does very well in these cases. Then courage becomes self-perpetuating; courage informs the tactics, and watching the tactics work will feed confidence and courage. It's calming and is the opposite of polarization.

What would you suggest to people in positions of authority who want to prevent a situation from becoming polarized?

In polarization, both sides believe that if they win—whether it be an election, an argument, or a school board vote—then the other side must obey them. What happens instead is that the winners face a world of resentment, with an opposition that blocks them at every turn.

This behavior can be understood by what sociologists call procedural justice. In procedural justice, people don't just automatically obey, but watch how an authority behaves. If they feel an authority is unjust, they may not comply, but resist. Procedural justice has three criteria:

- ♦ Does the authority have respect for human dignity?
- ♦ Do I have a voice in what happens to me?
- ♦ Does this authority care about my welfare?

Polarization goes against all three criteria. Those on the losing side feel demonized and humiliated. They may feel this new authority hates and despises them. They feel they will not be heard, will have no control over what will happen to them, and the authority has little or no concern for their welfare.

Those on the losing side will not cooperate. They will disobey, either openly or quietly, undermine the authority, and generally do what they can to guarantee that the authority fails. And the more the authority tries to demonize the other side and "win," the more this guarantees that the other side will not comply. It's a self-defeating pattern.

As it happens, women religious tend to do very well with procedural justice. You meet all three criteria: you feel it's your place to care about all sorts of people, including those who don't agree with you; you treat others with respect; and you are willing to listen. Most important, your actions are consistent with your words.

This is part of why women religious have emerged as a powerful religious voice. People don't always agree with what you do. But agree or not, they accept that sisters genuinely care, which lends a credibility missing from most authority.

As a society, how might we roll back this tendency to polarization? How might women religious leaders contribute to this effort?

Polarization tends to work at lightning speeds. The next time you hear someone get into an angry argument, tune out the words and listen to the pacing: it tends to be fast, explosive, quick on rebuttal. And the other side often fires back without listening at all.

The cognition researcher, Dr. Daniel Kahneman, wrote an excellent book called *Thinking, Fast and Slow*. He discovered our brains operate in two separate modes: fast thinking and slow thinking. Fast thinking uses very little of the brain's circuitry. It jumps to conclusions, convinced that it's right, and is largely impervious to its own mistakes. In fact, when fast thinking encounters a question it can't answer, it substitutes a simple question and answers that. It's a snapshot of polarized thinking.

But Kahneman found we have a second mode: slow thinking. Slow thinking uses much more brain circuitry. It's more complex, less clichéd, more inventive. It's also more work, so we tend not to do it. In fact, given a hard problem, slow thinking can typically find a better answer, but is rarely called in.

Women religious are unusually good at slow thinking. You're trained in contemplation, to sit with a question without jumping to conclusions. You school yourselves in discernment and depth, rather than sharp retorts to win an argument.

Since Vatican II, women religious have spent decades working together through tumultuous change. By all reports this was very hard, but it trained you to go for deep discernment. You did not want winners and losers; you wanted solid answers with lasting, high-quality results.

To get there, women religious engaged in communal contemplation, putting a difficult question before dozens, even hundreds of colleagues and considering it without arguing. This is a model of decision-making that's unlike anything we're used to in Western debates.

In working with women religious, I've noticed that rather than answer a difficult question, you may pause and go back to your committees or communities for discernment. I call it going back to the hive. It seems like it's one part crowd-sourcing and one part supercomputer.

Michelle Sommerville, a blogger, made a passing reference to convents as de facto think tanks. Consider that for a moment. Combine the sisters' firsthand knowledge of the problems of the world, your collaborative nature, and your contemplative skills, not to mention your strong education and ability to do more with less money than anyone else in the nation. This is an extraordinary resource.

It's a great idea to tap women religious as a think tank. It makes you wonder why no one thought of it before.

This is a moment when Catholic sisters have been pushed more into the public light and our positions on issues are more scrutinized and subject to criticism. What advice do you have for leaders who are operating in this more intense public light?

Polarized times can feel very strange: your best and brightest leaders come under attack, not for what they've done wrong, but for what they've done right. In fact, it can be tempting to limit your own strengths, hide your light under a bushel just so you won't be made a target. These feelings aren't unreasonable. Polarization repels talent. It drives away intelligent, dynamic people at the very time we need them most. Look at the public sector. The shortage of talent is killing us.

Benjamin Franklin was a talented soul in polarized times, and he took this approach: be tactful, even when tempers are high. When possible, give credit to others. Use humor when you can. Resist your temper; be kind. That's all wise. But never limit your own strengths. Embrace them. If others are uncomfortable with thoughtfulness or intelligence, they can cope. They can learn to meet you in dialogue. They're less fragile than you think.

What might leaders do when they recognize that fear is a significant factor in a polarizing situation?

In face of fear, breathe. Pray. Beware of a phenomenon called flooding, where adrenaline overwhelms the brain. Typical symptoms are whirling thoughts, feeling overwhelmed, and an inability to listen or find options. It's a chemical response, where parts of the brain essentially disconnect. It's human, of course, but not what we need in leaders.

Fear fuels polarization, and when our leaders are fearful, bad things happen. Fearful leaders make awful decisions. As Pat Farrell pointed out in her LCWR presidential address, these times call for fearlessness. Fearlessness, by the way, is not about rushing the barricades. That's impulse. The most impressive fearlessness holds steady, does the work, and watches for a thoughtful opening. It takes fearlessness not to force anyone's hand.

Be careful of your first reaction in polarized times. It usually comes from fear or anger, and it's rarely your best option. Timing itself is a gift, and a skill that can be developed. Like any strength, embrace it.

Dealing with conflict in a healthy, productive way takes courage. In a world where we don't have many heroes or role models in courage, how can we work on developing courage?

Tell your stories. A curious failing in healthy conflict is that people neglect to talk about themselves. Of course it's refreshing; rather the opposite of so much of what's out there. But the downside is that in healthy conflict, people say so little about themselves that they don't pass along enough basic information that other people can learn from their experiences.

Women religious have a wealth of experience they hardly mention. Some were active in Chile under Pinochet. Some went to Central America in the times of the death squads. They work in inner cities, around gangs, with aldermen. You have done extraordinary things under extraordinary circumstances. You tend to take this for granted. The rest of us need you to articulate how you did it.

In the West we've become jaded about leaders. We don't expect courage. Certainly there are few images of courage and older women. Yet you have courage in abundance. You may not think of yourselves that way; you may feel scared when you find yourself in a situation. But that's the secret: courageous people get scared. It's that they do courageous things anyway. Your version of courage is so often gracious, thoughtful, and unpretentious. We need that kind of courage in our leaders, and we need clear examples if we're ever to raise our expectations. We also need to know how it happened. Tell your stories.

17

Transformative Leadership in a Time of Public Crisis

Breege O'Neill, RSM

*Beginning in 1996, the Congregation of the Sisters of Mercy, Ireland, became the object of public criticism regarding abuses that are alleged to have occurred in the 1940s, 1950s, and 1960s at orphanages for which they were responsible. LCWR sought out a conversation with the congregational leader of these Sisters of Mercy, **Breege O'Neill, RSM**, who assumed leadership in 2000, about how she led her community through a time of public trial and humiliation. How does a leader help her organization's membership cope through such an experience? How can one make meaning while in the midst of a harsh and traumatic event? How can a leader allow an enormously difficult situation to become an agent of profound transformation for an organization?*

How did the public criticism of the Sisters of Mercy begin?

The public criticism began as a result of a television program, *Dear Daughter,* being screened in 1996 on RTE, our national TV station. The focus of this program was the story of one person's account of her life in an orphanage run by our congregation. The program resulted in weeks of negative media focus on the congregation and hostile public reaction. It was followed by a number of other television programs, including a four-part series called *States of Fear*, and also the publication of a number of books and newspaper articles, all describing the painful stories of individuals who spent their childhoods in orphanages and industrial schools run not only by Mercy Sisters but by various religious congregations in Ireland. The allegations in relation to the Sisters of Mercy focused on corporal punishment, a climate of harshness and exploitation. All these revelations came at a time of increased antipathy toward the Catholic Church in Ireland and the worldwide exposure of sexual abuse by clergy in the Catholic Church, and this is the context in which we have been seeking to respond.

What was your leadership team's response as the crisis began to develop?

The leadership team of 1994–2000 was made aware in advance of the screening of this program, and their concern was for those who had been in our institutions and for the members of our congregation. They took initial steps to respond to both. To prepare the sisters in advance of viewing the program they communicated as much information as they had. A public apology from the congregation was issued immediately after the *Dear Daughter* program.

They also immediately launched a confidential and independent Mercy-funded help line together with a counseling service for those who wished to avail themselves of it. Our congregational archives was expanded and developed to deal with requests from former residents for information and records, and a qualified psychologist was engaged to be available to those receiving personal records.

What was the public's response to this?

Initial efforts to respond to complainants in a pastoral way were viewed as being defensive. Those for whom it was intended rejected the very idea of a help line run by the congregation, and so the help line and counseling service were then staffed and run by a professional agency. This service has since been expanded to a service funded by the Conference of Religious of Ireland.

The ongoing stories in the media continued with features, analysis, and comment on a daily basis. It felt as if we were constantly reacting to negative publicity. This is quite different from what is happening presently around abuse issues in other countries where there is now a context. In our situation, the context was being created, and we were trying to react to it. In the immediate aftermath of the television program, civil lawsuits were initiated against the congregation by a number of people who had been in our institutions. The impact of all of this was overwhelming for us. It was a long way from how we saw and experienced ourselves up to this time.

How were your sisters coping at this point?

Initially the sisters were stunned and "paralyzed" by the media stories. We have generally refrained from speaking publicly through the media because of the fear of adding to the pain of former residents. We believed that their stories needed and deserved to be heard and that it was important that space was given for that. However, every time a new piece appeared in the media, we would have members asking, "Why aren't we defending ourselves?" And some who wanted to tell the "other story" were not listened to by the media.

The morale of the congregation plummeted. The feelings throughout the congregation ranged from confusion, anger, depression, to denial and grief. We moved through all of the stages of the grieving cycle, but we did not move neatly through them. We had the whole mix together of people experiencing different emotions. There were those who felt that this was a media-driven issue, more about money than hurt, all a product of a society with an agenda to rid itself of the power the Catholic Church held in Ireland.

How did the leadership team address this reality?

Leadership had to come to grips with their own feelings and responses and find a way to work with membership. Early on they had to clarify for themselves what non-negotiable values they wanted to hold in their interactions with all involved—those making allegations, those against whom allegations were being made, the media, as well as members of the congregation and all with whom we related. They articulated a congregational stance, which identified the following values: a desire for justice to all concerned, a commitment to search for the truth, and pastoral concern for all. These values have served as a template that we have used in each stage of the process.

A number of safe spaces were created throughout the congregation where members could talk about their feelings and reactions and their own experiences of hurt and oppression. This was made possible by a small group of sisters who were appointed to engage the congregation in a process of theological reflection around the question: What is God saying to us/asking of us in all the events that are unfolding? Initially, they used a series of reflections on the culture and society that prevailed in Ireland in the 1940s and '50s, the situation of women in society, the image of God and the theology of religious life that was prevalent, and the understanding of psychology that informed attitudes to children during that period. As well as providing the sisters with information to help them understand the context from which these allegations of abuse were emerging, this information also became the framework for theological reflection.

When you were elected leader, your congregation had been dealing with this issue for three and a half years. What was it like to assume leadership at that time?

In 2000, which was when I was elected to leadership in the congregation, the government had stepped in to search for a resolution. It delivered a comprehensive apology to those who had suffered, it set up a statutory Commission of Inquiry into Child Abuse, and it announced the setting up of a redress scheme by which compensation would be awarded. The religious orders were invited by the government to contribute to the redress scheme, and we along with other congregations responded positively to that invitation.

This issue had been live for the congregation for at least four years prior to my being elected leader. Of its nature it is a very complex and involved issue. It demanded hours of reading, briefing, questioning, trying to understand and get a hold on that complexity. Because we had been responsible for twenty-seven industrial schools/orphanages caring for more than eleven thousand children during the period in question, it was necessary to have a place where all of the ongoing information could be dealt with. We developed a project office that held and collated all the information centrally, and that engaged in ongoing research regarding the context and the developing situation.

At that time some sisters in the congregation were called to appear at the Commission of Inquiry, and their care was a matter of priority for us. In collaboration with our provincial leadership teams, supports were put in place to care for the needs of those sisters and all sisters who had worked in child care throughout their lives. We had ongoing meetings with all our membership to give them information, to continue reflection, and to deal with all sorts of feelings. We did this side by side with all the other aspects of the life of the congregation with which we had to deal, but we consistently kept our attention focused on this issue.

How did you find that your sisters responded?

Gradually, over time, many of our sisters began to move beyond anger and denial into a space where they could engage with the allegations without becoming unduly discouraged.

One of the greatest gifts for us on this journey was the grace to own in the present the truth of our collective failure to always live the compassion and tenderness that was the Mercy ideal that we professed.

Lest it sound like we made this very neat spiritual journey, all of the time we had to deal with anger, with our sisters who felt that we were the target for every negative reaction that anybody wanted to make, and with those who felt that we weren't doing enough to stand up for the good name of the congregation. Holding in tension the trauma of those who recall being treated harshly and the pain of our own women against whom allegations of abuse have been made has not been easy. The reality has been that we have had to learn as we went along, and the story continued to change and take new, unexpected turns.

Were you able to help your sisters make meaning of what was happening?

We were able to do this in a number of ways. Consistent efforts were made to inform, update, form, and educate all our sisters in relation to all the complexities of this issue, particularly as new and different facets continued to emerge. We have found that the consistent sharing of information has been hugely helpful in reducing anxiety. We tried to move from a place where individual sisters felt blamed to a place where together, as a congregation, we were taking responsibility for our past on a basis that was broader than this issue alone. We addressed the system of religious life in the past where often humanity was sacrificed.

We also moved this from the past to the present. We asked if this was just something about the past or if it had a question and a challenge for the present. What is the merciful thing we are being called to in the present? Where might we be failing to be merciful in our relationships with each other in community? We took it as a conversion call to ourselves. It changed the meaning of this issue from being a crisis over which we had no control to being a faith call to look at our lives.

We gradually realized that we were engaging the shadow side of the congregation at this time, and while this was painful for us, we knew that there was potential in it. We were led into a path of intense reflection, as individuals, as leadership, and as a congregation.

A major learning for us in relation to ministry has been that people who worked in the ministry of childcare in the past were grossly overworked because of an approach to need that meant we could never turn anybody away. This often meant that we let the state off the hook in its responsibility to provide adequate resources.

Were there any scripture images that you used in theological reflection that were particularly helpful?

Scripture stories were an ongoing source of formation and nourishment for us. Whenever we gathered our sisters we began our meetings with reflection on a particular scripture story. I am thinking in particular of stories such as the woman at the well, the burning bush, the storm at sea, the story of Jonah, and the appearance of Jesus to the disciples on the sea of Tiberius. We asked: What is it that we have to step aside to look at? How can we take off our shoes of prestige and stand barefoot and vulnerable? Those images and stories helped us a lot, and as time went on the invitation of Christ after the resurrection, "Cast your nets to starboard" called us to trust anew the God who was guiding us.

Where have you seen the reflection process take your congregation?

Last year during Lent we took three biblical stories from Luke 15: The Lost Coin, The Lost Sheep, and The Lost Son/ Daughter and engaged in reflection as a congregation. That brought us all to a place of action. We looked at what steps toward reconciliation we were being called to. For a long time the form of that step was not clear, but once we realized that an apology spoken directly to our former residents through the medium of the media that stood on its own with no agenda except a sincere desire to apologize and be reconciled was the way to go, we walked it. We knew that we had apologized in 1996. We came to a realization that that apology could not be heard then because of an emotional wall that existed at the time. This time we wanted to say we were truly sorry. We felt it. We moved to a place of really experiencing heartfelt sorrow ourselves as we learned to stand in the shoes of a young child separated from family and left alone in a big institution.

We could only trust in God that the apology would be heard this time in the spirit out of which it was made. Out of that place, we made a congregational statement of apology in May 2004. The impact that the statement had on the total congregation was a freeing one. We could now own that people had been hurt in our institutions and that we were deeply regretful and pained by that.

How did you make the public statement?

We called a press conference and delivered our apology there. While the press conference itself was quite difficult, the reporting of the statement in the media was very positive and those for whom it was intended welcomed it and accepted our apology.

Why do you think it was heard in 2004?

It was heard for a number of reasons. Over time a sense of balance had come into the picture in the public domain. Positive stories were being reported, a number of false allegations were being acknowledged. The redress scheme set up by the government had become operational. The fact that people were getting redress contributed to a change in the public climate. For ourselves we also realized that we had not really listened to the complaints of people who had been in our orphanages. Some had said, "You never acknowledged that anything that we were saying was true." We took note of that and we began to make more contact with individuals and groups informally but consistently and to listen to them. Now we are formally and informally trying to build on that. This situation is in a different place for us and I don't think it could be, if we, as a congregation, had not made the journey ourselves and tried to find our own soul in all of it.

How, as a leader, did you keep the work involved in this issue in balance with all of the other leadership responsibilities?

The need to take time to pray, reflect, and process the unfolding reality was very necessary and also very strengthening for me. A lot of time was spent consulting and meeting with leaders and members in the congregation, with leaders in other congregations, and with the many and varied people and groups involved in this whole area. The structures and networks already in place to carry forward this work were invaluable at this time. These were some of the steps that basically assured that this issue did not consume the total life of leadership.

How did you keep your spirits up?

Once again I would have to say that faith and trust in God was our greatest anchor. I believe that it was this that helped us to engage the situation not as a constant interruption of life but as a call to conversion. We created ongoing space for reflection for ourselves as a team, and we engaged leadership and membership in this reflection. Now, to say that sounds as if it never got us down, but it did. We felt the burden, and at times it seemed unending and insurmountable.

What, if anything, would you do differently if this happened again now?

When this happened, we were reactive and we were fearful at first. We felt besieged by the media and the victim groups. We were utterly at sea as to how to respond. If we were to start now, we would seek to really hear what was being said and be proactive. We would trust our own gut pastoral response, take more risk in trying to reach out to those who were hurt.

Has this experience had any long-range effects on your congregation?

We are now in a completely different place from where we were in 1996. Then we had just amalgamated twenty-seven individual units of Sisters of Mercy. We were very upbeat as a congregation, and we were going to change the world! We were riding the crest of a wave at that time. This crisis has brought us to our knees and to a place where we are much more conscious of our own failings. We are conscious of our contributions as well, but in a much more humble way.

This has been a time of purification for us, a time when the pedestals on which society had placed us have been toppled, when we have been marginalized and rejected, when we have had to endure seeing the work we did being disregarded, our good name being tarnished, and our self-confidence being eroded. In the past the mirror that reflected our identity to us was the mirror of success and being well thought of and respected. Now that mirror has been shattered, and from the shattered fragments we have to find ourselves again.

Would you say that this has been such a powerful change because it came from beyond yourselves?

Absolutely. Both the trigger that set us on this journey of change and the guidance that sustained us on the journey

came from beyond ourselves. Since Vatican II our renewal efforts have been about what we choose to change. However,
something like this is not about what we choose, but rather it
is about being changed by and responding in faith to situations
not of our own choosing, and which, if we had a choice in the
matter, would not be where we would want to go.

I would have to say too that it was often in reflecting back
on our journey that we recognized how we were being changed
and that the actions we took were by the grace of God rather
than by a clearly prepared plan of our own. Over time we
chose the journey into restorative justice rather than that of
retributive justice. We cannot take the credit for consciously
making that choice. We were led into it by the spirit of God,
responding a step at a time to what we believed was the next
right thing to do. Those who made the journey with us, including a former resident who challenged us as a congregation
"to find ourselves where we lost ourselves," also were a blessing to us. We celebrate our change very humbly by acknowledging "that God has done great things for us."

*If you were to sit down with a leader who was just beginning this
kind of journey with her own congregation, what advice would
you give her?*

I would say hold your own integrity as a group. Try to listen to
all the different voices that are coming forward, and especially
seek out the ones that are not being heard. Get the full facts
in relation to each situation, source all the advice you need, be
as informed as you can possibly be about the substance of allegations, and then be proactive in your response, engaging all
the help needed to do this. Respond compassionately to complainants, holding reconciliation as an overreaching value and
desire rather than have media or legal people dictate to you
how to respond. Be attentive to the needs of membership and
also encourage and support them to engage the faith journey

that the situation presents. Use the media proactively. Pray, reflect, discern personally and with your team and the wider leadership, and avail of supports like spiritual direction, supervision, and personal care.

Above all, don't try to sidestep the darkness that is involved in walking this journey, but trust that it can bring you to a new place.

LEADERSHIP
AMONG FUTURE GENERATIONS

18

Forming Leaders
for These Changing Times

Eileen Campbell, RSM, and Nancy Schreck, OSF

Recognizing the rapid change occurring in the world today, LCWR began developing a formation program that helps its members practice leadership in a manner that is effective and relevant for these times. The program, Leadership Pathways, provides education, support, and inspiration to LCWR members as they strive to be the spiritual leaders needed for the challenges of this moment in history. Two of the women involved in the creation of this program offer their

Eileen Campbell, RSM

Nancy Schreck, OSF

insights on why leadership needs to be different today, some of the skills leaders ought to develop, and why ongoing formation is critical for any leader today. The interviewees are **Nancy Schreck, OSF**, *then president of the Sisters of St. Francis of Dubuque and a former LCWR president; and* **Eileen Campbell, RSM**, *a member of the leadership team of the Institute of the Sisters of Mercy of the Americas.*

What do you see happening in religious life today that points to a need for a leadership formation program? What makes this time in religious life different from even the recent past?

Eileen: Before we can begin to talk about what is happening in religious life today, we need to talk about what is happening in the world and universe. We are living in very different times in terms of values, the economy, understandings of commitment, the pace at which we live, even the accessories we use—all of which impact our lives. In light of this, I think the desire and the need we have to deepen our contemplative spirituality is critical for us in religious life. We are even more drawn to contemplation because of what is happening in the world and, at the same time, there is a hunger among many people in the world for this same experience of contemplation. I think what LCWR has been doing in these past years as it invites us into deeper experiences of contemplation highlights that desire and need in the world. So it is critically important that we learn the skills and practices that can support leaders for living and acting from a contemplative stance in the midst of a rapidly changing world.

Nancy: I agree, and would add that there is an institutional decline occurring in the world today as well, including the decline of religions and religious institutions. As Eileen said, we need to clearly articulate the deep spiritual core out of which we come, because this is what people are hungry for. They are disillusioned with institutions of religion and yet have this great longing for spirituality.

Within religious life, we are becoming lighter, more agile, and freer from many of our ministry commitments that held our whole lives in place previously. This puts us in a great place for articulating the essence of our lives. We are finally getting stripped of all the protective layers that we have been able to carry for so long and that are just now going away. We are forced to look to one another and ask what we want to be about. We are now getting small enough that we can have these conversations together. I also think that we have greater clarity about our need for corporate witness. In the past we could rely on our numbers for corporate witness, but now we need to ask how we can best use our influence as smaller groups. This is an area that needs to be probed as we think about leadership.

Eileen: It's important to think about what is happening beyond religious life. Leadership in the United States and in other countries is very different since it is no longer all in the hands of a hierarchical government. Just look at the Occupy Movement. I believe we have to think about this in relation to religious life. I believe we still need elected leaders, but we have to learn how to better model shared leadership. Members want to be involved, and they want to be a part of naming the essence of religious life. So there is a call to leaders to learn how to engage the members and share leadership and decision-making. And I think this all connects with what we are learning in terms of how the universe works. As we become more aware of the interdependence that exists within the universe, it's natural that we would see that same awareness growing in our religious communities.

Nancy: We experienced this kind of shift in leadership in our community a couple of years ago when we began to reflect on some of our congregation structures. We looked at some of the structures that held us in the past and asked, "Are these working for us now?" For example, we looked at our area groups, and each had a representative who participated in a central assembly. We did away with that, and when we did some people became nervous about who was going to represent them. But we no longer needed a representational form of leadership. Now we can all be in the same room at the same time. So now we have to learn how to engage everyone in processes of problem-solving and direction-setting.

What are some of the other challenges facing women religious leaders that are significant to this conversation?

Eileen: I think one of the challenges is learning how to lead in the midst of so much diversity in thought and opinion.

How do we, as leaders, learn to have—and facilitate others in having—conversations where there are great differences of opinion and learn to come to resolutions together? We find ourselves in many situations where we are with people who have differing viewpoints on the church, faith expressions, theological issues, and different understandings of ministry and priorities. How do we learn to live with this kind of diversity? How do we learn to accept differences rather than aim for uniformity?

Nancy: I have been thinking about how we can live less and less like silos. As we bring religious life into the future, I think we can't rely just on learning from ourselves. We need to be learning from all kinds of different organizations. This is not to say that we are not good enough, or that we don't have the answers. It's rather that the answers never lie in just one perspective or one group. So I think we need a broad menu of leadership conversation in order to learn what we need to know for this kind of time. We can't afford not to be in partnership with others who have commitments to the issues that concern us. So, for example, if we are looking at issues of immigration or peacemaking or any other matter of justice, are we talking with people who are not just like us? This is especially important as we become smaller in numbers. We could easily also become more and more isolated and more concerned about just taking care of ourselves. While I don't think this is where we are as women religious, diminishment can make people turn inward. We have become used to relying on other religious, so it might be a little stretch for us to think about finding new partners. Maybe our best partner in some new project is not the group of sisters on the other side of town, but maybe the city water department, or other entities like this.

Eileen: Our leadership team recently participated in a workshop that was attended by fifty men and women who represented a diversity of cultures from all over the world. We discovered through a process of conversation and asking one another questions that we all have the same vision for sustainability. We concluded at the end that one of the steps for promoting sustainability is to invite around your table the least likely partners.

Nancy: And this is just what Leadership Pathways is trying to do. Part of the design of this program includes inviting to the table a variety of leaders from other walks of life who have important insights for us.

Eileen: This is a different way of looking at collaboration. In the past we would say, "This is what we want to do and who can support us in doing it?" We looked for people who thought like we do. Now we are saying, "This is our vision, this is why we want to do this, and who might want to do it with us—and not just support us while we do it?" This is another leadership skill for these times: How do we involve other people in our lives and ministries? How do we empower leaders to take the risk of inviting the least likely people around the table?

What are some of the other skills that women religious need to be effective leaders at this unique time?

Nancy: I think one skill is learning to be multilingual. I don't mean speaking another language like Spanish or French, but rather learning to be conversant with people of very diverse viewpoints.

Eileen: I would agree, and I also think that understanding organizational development is key. Businesses, banks, corporations, non-profits are all looking into what makes for effective leadership and how to use that leadership to influence organizational structures. We need to understand historically what is happening in other organizations in society as well as in our own.

Another critical skill is learning how to lead in an interdependent way. This would involve learning how to engage and involve others—whether that be our own members, our boards, or whomever we invite to the table with us. How do we engage together for the common good and not feel as leaders that we have to do it all ourselves?

Nancy: Right—and it is not about disengaging as leaders, but about engaging in very purposeful sharing. Better results happen when the circle is broader and more people are invested.

Eileen: Another skill that I see you practicing, Nancy, is thinking out of the box. I always wonder if that is a skill one can learn or if it is just a gift some people have naturally. I don't personally have out-of-the-box ideas, but I have an out-of-the-box attitude. I may not know how to do the out-of-the-box things, but I can sure recognize when an out-of-the-box idea is needed or when one is proposed. So I think an important skill is learning to develop a comfortableness with out-of-the-box ideas and also to develop skills for helping others not only to think out-of-the-box, but also act on the ideas that are different.

Nancy: I think the skill you are naming, Eileen, is the skill of option-thinking. The hardest people for me to interact with are those who can think of only one way to do things. In option-thinking, we might start with one "right answer," and then push ourselves to think up three, or four, or even ten more.

Eileen: In a recent workshop with Peter Senge, one of the participants said, "If you have two options, when you choose one, you then lose the other." Senge said, "Why would you have to do that?" He helped us move beyond our old either-or patterns of thinking to more creative thinking that encourages us to see more possibilities.

Nancy: This relates to another skill of learning, to see leadership as a blend of both the management of the organization and the tending to the vision for moving the organization forward. It seems that the work of closing down buildings or phasing out programs is taking an inordinate amount of the energy and time of leaders and members. How do leaders not just stay with doing that kind of work or with work they are good at, but rather find a balance? I think this is part of what you were saying, Eileen, about learning what organizational development entails. I could think I am doing organizational development when I taking down buildings, getting everything in my community right-sized, finding the right combination of our assets and investments, and all the rest. But that is only a piece of the work. The poetic language being used today involves learning to be both a hospice worker and midwife at the same time.

Eileen: It's important to remember too that while leaders need to attend to both aspects, they don't have to be expected to have the skills and gifts to do it all.

Nancy: Which is another skill: knowing how to access what you need.

We often hear leaders say that one of the reasons they put most of their time into the practical tasks of leadership is that they don't know how to exactly go about doing the visionary parts. How do you see Leadership Pathways helping people learn how to engage in the inspirational and visionary dimensions of leadership?

Eileen: Although the program might address these dimensions in a presentation, or a video, or a reading, I think where people will really be helped is through the mentoring and peer support components of Leadership Pathways. So much of leaders' time is spent at meetings where they are discussing a situation and what needs to be done to address that situation. Mentors and those in peer support groups are attentive to listening to the leader as a person and what her hopes are and what she might need to do to fulfill those hopes. Mentors help people realize their goals and stretch them. When a leader works with a mentor she cannot stay where she is—and most leaders want this; they don't want to not grow. But sometimes we just need someone to listen to us, and we don't always have that—leaders least of all.

Nancy: An important part of Leadership Pathways is providing a safe place for me to articulate my own deepest desires and my community's deepest desires. And sometimes I don't even know what those desires are until I hear myself say them aloud. I can read books and I can go to workshops, but it's not until I have to articulate the vision myself that it becomes clear. And I cannot speak that vision to my whole community until I have heard myself put it into words.

I think mentoring and peer support are particularly important for these times because we are making a path by walking it; we don't yet know how to lead for such a different time. Brother Philip Pinto said recently that although religious life has gone through times of great shifts in culture and society, we may be the first generation to be very conscious of the kinds of shifting grounds we are on. So we might be conscious of the shifts, but we aren't clear about how to move and if we are walking together. But we know that we have a greater opportunity to make a path if we make it together, rather than in isolation.

Aside from the mentoring and peer support dimensions of the program, how else do you see Leadership Pathways addressing some of the challenges to leadership that you have both noted?

Eileen: I think the program mirrors just what we are saying we need. We are saying we need help in thinking out of the box and we need to connect and learn from and involve people from outside of our usual circles of religious life. Leadership Pathways will provide people with a variety of resources, and some of them may be from places and people who are not the "usual suspects."

What have you personally done for your own leadership formation that helps underscore your conviction that such formation is critical for religious life leaders today?

Nancy: Our team begins our monthly meetings with what we call the big question discussion. We take turns each month in choosing an article for the team to read that has nothing at all to do with religious life. It might be about trends in business or industry, or about spiritual movements or other topics. After we spend time discussing the article, we conclude by asking, "Now what might that have to do with our leadership?" So, this is a way to stretch our thinking, and to get us to read broadly about movements in other areas, and then to see what we can take from that to help our work.

Eileen: Some of the things that we did as a team that were helpful include working with a good facilitator for the team and with a coach for a while. Coaches can be expensive, but we were able to negotiate, and our individual sessions with the coach were life-changing. We have also had in-services and gone to workshops on topics that involve more than just religious life per se. I also make spiritual direction a priority, and I have taken advantage of a mentor—just checking in from time to time with a person whose wisdom I value who has helped me to look at things in different ways.

I think the most important thing is choosing time to do what we need to do. So it may be taking time to read, or go to a workshop. It may be just to take a day off and go walk in the park.

Nancy: Several years ago I heard someone say on National Public Radio that one of the problems today for organizational leaders is that when they go away, they take their cell phones, laptops, and everything else with them. The person being interviewed said that the most important things leaders can do is go away and not keep any connection to the work they are doing. Very few of us in religious life leadership do this—and I am not sure that is a good thing. I loved when you said, Eileen, we may need to just go and take a walk in the park. That may be just as important as taking time for studying some critical issue. I also think that exposing ourselves to other people and other organizations is key. If I am only interacting with women religious, my world is going to be too small.

What recommendations would you make to leaders as they con-sider participating in Leadership Pathways?

Eileen: We need to make it a priority. This is not an extra thing we do; it is a responsibility and part of our accountability to our congregations. We owe it to our congregations to de-velop ourselves into the role our members have called us to. So, on one hand, this is about ourselves, but we are so inter-connected that what affects us is going to affect others. What we get out of this program will have a positive impact on everyone else—the women in our congregations, the people with whom we work, the other leaders with whom we journey.

Nancy: I love what you're saying, Eileen. We are doing this for the life of the whole. I would also say that we can't afford not to do something like this. It is such a new time that we can-not just do what we have seen done before. That is probably how most of us judge whether or not we could do leadership. We look at what leaders before us did and say, "In some way I could do that." But this is a whole new time and there aren't many models out there. We are making the way by walking it. So it is critical for us to be in environments where what is needed for the future is explored.

I would also stress that Leadership Pathways is not just for people who are new to leadership. I was in leadership from 1992 to 2000. My congregation was an entirely different or-ganization then, and how I did leadership was very different then. I think I had intuitions that it would be different now, but I don't think I realized the depth of difference.

Eileen: I am in my second consecutive term of leadership and I see great differences from even just the first term. Each chap-ter gives us a new focus, and the focus of our last chapter was very different from the one previous to it. The focus determines what skills I need this time and where my energies will go. I never expected to find in a second term the degree to which we are being stretched and called to think and act differently. So I would say that there is no such thing as a program just for new leaders. There are some things that need to be addressed when you are brand new, but we are never finished growing and learning. I actually think that the more experience you have had, the greater the desire to develop and engage more.

I also think that we need to look at leadership development differently. It is not like staying updated in a profession where you are required to learn new theories and skills. This is a call. We are being called to become the best persons we can be for the good of the whole. This means we are being called to continue to form and shape and reshape and develop. It is a privilege as well as a responsibility. New leaders need to learn specific things, but it doesn't stop for us after that. It actually begins after that.

Is there anything else you would like to say?

Eileen: Yes, I want to say that if anyone has a doubt as to whether they should engage in Leadership Pathways, call us. Call any one of us on the committee. As we have worked on developing this program, we experienced the energy of people coming together with this common hope for the future and see this as a way of going forward. So, let us share that energy with you.

Nancy: I would like people to realize that while this is a very challenging time, it's really a fun time. It is exciting to learn about new things and find new ways of being and doing leadership. This does not have to be a burden—like something we have to get figured out—but it can be an enjoyable, creative experience.